...Because of Jesus

TK Dunn

Energion Publications
Cantonment, Florida
2025

ISBN: 978-1-63199-950-5
eISBN: 978-1-63199 951-6

Energion Publications
1241 Conference Rd
Cantonment, FL 32533

pubs@energion.com

Arthur Julius Dunn

*May you come to saving faith at a tender age
and follow the Master ever thereafter...*

...Because of Jesus.

Table of Contents

Acknowledgements

I want to express gratitude to CIU and TBC for the privilege of presenting these talks and for their support of the gospel ministry in their communities. Being surrounded by so many different people who are each uniquely and passionately captivated by the gospel of Jesus continues to be a source of inspiration, encouragement, and joy to me.

A special thanks to Henry Neufeld and *Energion* for this second publication with them. If you find this book enjoyable, I hope that you might consider *"Take and Eat": From Fall To Feast* as your next purchase. Henry's enthusiasm for healthy spiritual resources that will disciple the church makes working with him a pleasure.

To my family across the oceans, thank you. I love you and am thankful that the Lord, in his mercy, has called each of you to him through his grace.

To Yesenia, my love, thank you for putting up with my many projects, ideas, and work. Your journey into motherhood has helped my love for you blossom into something larger and newer than I even knew was possible. Thank you for making our home a place of worship, peace, and joy where I can be productive, goofy, and yours.

Invocation

Sovereign Lord, thank you for sending your only begotten Son, perfect in nature, one in substance with you, to the earth to take on flesh. Thank you for the mercy that accepted his death in our place and for the provision of a new life in him and the new creation.

Lord Jesus, we worship you as the Suffering Servant and the Lamb of God who was slaughtered by the world that the lost may be found, the dead may live, and the darkness turned to light. We are utterly unworthy of your grace and mercy, but we are so thankful you were obedient to the point of death on the cross.

Holy Spirit, we praise you for your glorious and patient ministry in each of us. So often we are deaf to your guidance and blind to your work, but you consistently intercede for us and continue to conform us into the likeness and image of our elder brother, Jesus. We submit to you.

I confess my own frailty and weakness; I am a sinner. But, like Jonah, you use broken people to amazing and glorious effect, not because of us, but in spite of us. I pray that you, Triune Lord, would let the words of these pages bring honor and glory to your name. Use them in the heart and mind of each reader to instill a deeper love for you, a greater passion for your gospel, and a broader appreciation of the work of Christ for each of us. Use it to lead souls to salvation that you may be glorified by new voices.

To the glory of the Father. By the work of the Spirit.

Because of Jesus.

Constantinopolitan Creed (AD 381)

This is the second creed that the early church formulated in an attempt to try to define the language and theology around the Trinity and the Person of Jesus. This creed is universally accepted by all Trinitarians who uphold the orthodox understanding of God as Triune and Christ as the Word-made-flesh. As you reflect on this incredible, ancient, and unifying creed, I hope that you will subtly hear the voices of billions of believers who have assented to these glorious truths over the last 1600 years since it was codified.

We repeat it with them. We confess it with them. We believe it with them. And together we form part of that incredible choir of Christians who profess that Christ is God, Christ is our Elder Brother, Christ is risen, and that Christ is returning.

We believe in one God, the Father Almighty, Maker of heaven and earth, and of all things visible and invisible.

And in one Lord Jesus Christ, the only-begotten Son of God, begotten of the Father before all worlds, Light of Light, very God of very God, begotten, not made, consubstantial with the Father; by whom all things were made;

Who for us men, and for our salvation, came down from heaven, and was incarnate by the Holy Ghost and the virgin Mary, and was made man; He was crucified for us under Pontius Pilate, and suffered, and was buried, and the third day He rose again, according to the Scriptures, and ascended into heaven, and sits on the right hand of the Father. From there He shall come again, with glory, to judge the living and the dead; whose kingdom shall have no end!

And in the Holy Spirit, the Lord and giver of life, who proceeds from the Father and the Son, and together with the Father and the Son, together is worshipped and glorified, who spoke by the prophets.

In one holy and universal church; we acknowledge one Baptism for the remission of the sins; we look for the resurrection of the dead, and the life of the world to come.

Amen.

Introduction

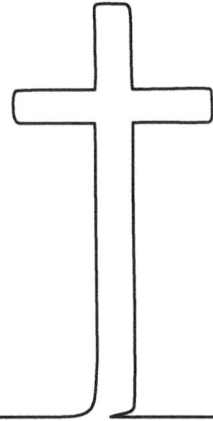

This book came about as a sermonette I presented at Columbia International University after a tragedy had hit our campus. The first one that I preached was '*Because of the Resurrection*' and it suggested to me that it would be beneficial to flesh out a series on the life, death, resurrection, and ascension of Jesus in such a way that believers could be enriched by grasping how the theology of Christ's work can apply to us today. I then preached the series at Tabernacle Baptist Church as an Easter series.

There is certainly no shortage of books on Christ's ministry. What sets this one apart, perhaps, is that I have endeavored to deliberately maintain the more informal preaching style rather than adapt the messages into a formal literary prose. Thus, at times, there may be sentences that lack a clause or a predicate and grammar may at times be less strict than would normally be the case, but I hope that will convey the sense of pace, enthusiasm, and dynamism that a sermon would produce. These chapters are each designed to be read and listened to as living reflections on the work of Jesus brought to bear on our lives where we are, in whatever circumstances we find ourselves, so that we can be encouraged to move forwards in faith and with Christ. The goal, I pray, is that by reading this little book, your knowledge of Christ will grow and your love for Christ will expand.

The first chapter will take us through the wondrous implications of the incarnation of God the Son. As we reflect on the incarnation, we will be confronted with why we *needed* God to take on our human condition. This will establish the foundational theological issue of humanity: sin. We are at war with God and need restoration but we are completely incapable of achieving that by ourselves. We need something, someone, external to us both individually and as a race. God answered our problem by sending Jesus.

In chapter two, we will look at the utter wickedness of rebellious man as we murdered the Messiah. The crucifixion, in all its gory horror will be revealed as the glory of Christ whose obedience was necessary to bring about the satisfaction of God's judgement, the defeat of Satan's rebellion, and the certainty of sin's ruination.

Chapter three will discuss the incredible reality of the resurrection of Christ and walk though aspects of the implications of the resurrection. By considering how it changes everything and establishes a new creational paradigm, we will see that there is so much often unsaid about the resurrection that can inspire deeper devotion.

The final chapter will gaze in wonder at the ascension. By considering Christ's exaltation and the Great Commission, we will we comforted by the glorious truths that Christ has conquered, he is risen, he is reigning, and he is returning. Because he is reigning and returning, we can be obedient to his calling in the meantime. We go in his strength, by his Spirit, to fulfil his mission, knowing that he will return with might, majesty, and finality. And when he does, all will be made right; evil will be vanquished, and God will be all in all.

If, afterwards, you can join in our motto to *Grow in Christ and Go with Christ*, I will consider it a success.

Any errors herein belong to me alone.
Soli Deo Gloria.

Chapter One:

...Because of the Incarnation

[John 1:1] *In the beginning was the Word, and the Word was with God, and the Word was God.*

Introduction

I'm always hungry. Especially now I'm "on a diet." Or that's what I often tell myself. It usually doesn't last terribly long. But when I'm "on a diet"? Well, suddenly, all I can think about, dream about, daydream about is food. Especially the *forbidden* foods like chips, fries, greasy cheeseburgers, and, joy of joys, *pizza*! Now that I'm dieting, carbs and fried food never smelt so good.

As a professor in a college, I'm often in the school cafeteria, where I get to dish all kinds of food onto my plate. Mac 'n' Cheeseburger chow mein, with a side of fries and curry sauce, anyone? I do often temper my gluttonous carbohydrate diet with a salad, of course. Admittedly, it's the last portion I eat...if there's room to spare.

But I have to confess that there's a bigger reason why I love eating in our school cafeteria. Beyond the mesmerizing culinary concoctions I can produce, there's something that I find quite *unique* about what happens in our school cafeteria. Students don't realize just quite how rare their experience is in our college campus.

But me? I've been to universities in Britain and America. I've been to them as an undergraduate and as a postgraduate. In fact, I've been to so many universities that there's a name for people like me: *Nerd*. I know my way around a college campus, and I especially know my way around a college cafeteria.

But at my college there is this fascinating phenomenon that is relatively distinct about our university.

Seated, in the cafeteria, amidst all of those rowdy bunch?

Are professors.

Not only the professors.

But the Provost. The Deans.

Even the President. Of the entire university!

Seated amongst the students. Laughing. Chatting. Advising. Even being teased! In no other college campus that I've been to, have I seen such a...spectacle. And it's a wonderful thing because it creates a culture of communication and of mutual respect. It allows students to bring any objections or concerns or (more often) confusions to their professors and, over a meal, they cultivate a relationship of respect, of valuing education, and of friendship. These friendships last well beyond the terminus of their academic studies at college. The cafeteria provides a culture where cultivating a joy of learning extends beyond the classroom and into the lives of both students and faculty (and even the deans and provost and president).

And the fact that professors sit with their students for lunch is not because we're too academic and can't do the practical thing of making a packed lunch for ourselves.

No!

Spoiler alert, *we love grabbing lunch with students*. Just as I hope, your elders and deacons love spending time and eating with you! Why? Because we're *eager* to invest in one another. To share life together over a meal is to replicate so much of Jesus and Paul's day-to-day ministry, isn't it? Doing life together, teaching, discipling, answering questions is a privilege for young and old alike.

Well, now, even as my Mac 'n' Cheeseburger is in your mind and making your tummy grumble, I want you to hold onto that image. That thought. About our college cafeteria. Where students eat with professors, provosts, and president.

Because in this chapter, we're going to talk about one of the most important, the most incredible, the most multiverse-breaking, earth-shattering, celestial paradoxes that has *ever* happened!

We're going to think about Christmas. No matter when you're reading this, it's not too long until Christmas, is it? It can never come soon enough, can it? Especially if you have, or indeed if you are, young enough to still be enamored by the tinsel, and lights, and snow, and decorations, and presents, and random foods we only eat at that time of year.

I love Christmas, and I'm sure that most of you do, too. Of course, in America we get to celebrate *two* diabetes-inducing holidays, not just one. So that's marvelous, isn't it?

But in Britain, where I come from, we don't have Thanksgiving. Thus, we throw *everything* at Christmas. All our winter-induced grumpiness and isolation is tempered by the fact that Christmas is coming. That winter break is such an exciting one, because it's more than just a break from classes, textbooks, assignments, and work. There's feasting. Family. Friends. There are parties. Pageantry. Presents.

Yet, so often it is the case that amidst all the distractions, even though we *try* to remember, we *fail* to *truly reflect* on the glory. The majesty. The wonder. The barely believable. That God. Became man.

God Became Man

[John 1:1] *In the beginning was the Word, and the Word was with God, and the Word was God.*

[2] *He was in the beginning with God.*

[3] *All things were made through Him, and without Him was not anything made that was made.*

We start here because we must remember that the Word, who is the second Person of the Trinity, is God.

The Word Is God

John starts this Gospel and the *very* first thing you should think is, "Oooh. That sounds a lot like Genesis!" You're right: "In the Beginning, God created the heavens and the earth." Thus opens the first verse in the whole Bible. The parallels are *intentional*, as well as *essential*.

In Genesis, we're introduced to the *God who creates*. Now, in John, we're introduced to the *Word who redeems*. In a way, John's giving us a new Genesis, explaining in greater depth and with more clarity what happened at creation. He is completing our knowledge of the beginning. Or, technically, before the beginning.

The phrase "in the beginning" that John uses at the very start of his biography of Jesus actually carries the meaning of "*at* the beginning." Effectively, John is telling us that the *Word* of God, who is also identified as the Son of God? He is *eternal*.

In verse 3, John uses very clear language to point out that *what* the Son creates? Well, it had a start date. It *was created*. Everything that the Son created began when he created it. Nothing that the Word created could pre-exist him. If it did, he couldn't have created it.

In contrast, however? The Word? He simply "was." He *wasn't* created. He was just there. *Before* creation, the Son *was*. In other words, the phrase "in the beginning was" really carries the meaning of something like "when all things began, the Word already was."

By making this point, John is doing something amazing here. Rather than speaking of the Word as a *philosophical idea* like the Greek philosophers or simply a *thing* like the Hebrew theologians, John tells us that the Word is a *person*. This is profound. It's often lost to us in our modern world and in our modern thinking because we're so familiar with the Christmas story. But John is breaking new ground for his readers. He isn't *inventing* the doctrine or the idea; but, under the inspiration of the Holy Spirit, he's clarifying and revealing this truth to us.

Thus, we are *now* able to see that the Father spoke in Genesis 1 but it was the Word who *caused* creation to exist. The Father spoke, the Son was the agent of creation, and the Spirit animated or gave life to creation. Creation is a Triune act. John tells us that the Word *was* the creator.

But this only makes sense if the Word *is* God. Which is exactly what John says next: "The Word," he says, "was God." So we see that the Word is God and the Word creates as God. It might appear mindboggling, and in a way, it *is* mindboggling. Yet, in the simplest terms, all that we can use to describe God can be said of the Father and of the Son and of the Spirit. God is holy. God is love. God creates. God redeems. God is just. Each of those adjectives can be said equally of Father, Son, or Spirit.

But John *also* tells us that the Word was *with* God. This means that there's a *distinction* between God the Father, and God the Son (and God the Spirit, though that distinction is not directly in view in this passage). As the Triune God, the Father and the Son is One God with all the attributes of the divine nature applying truly and wholly to each person.

And yet.

The Father and the Son are *not* the same person. They are *one God*, but the Son is *not* the Father, nor is the Father the Son. God is Trinity. He is three persons in one Being. James White talks about God as one What and three Whos. God is not schizophrenic. He's not divided into three parts. He's not three separate beings. But he is three distinct persons. And each person takes upon himself specific tasks or work or operations.

And John tells us that the Word? Is God. And that is *good* news for us. God the Son, eternal, glorious, majestic, holy, creator of *all* things. He's all powerful because *he is God*.

✞ Application: Jesus Has the Power to Help

If we apply this, Christian, we realize that, *because* Jesus is God, we can call out to him in our weakness. In despair. In our trials. In our traumas.

And he is able to help us.

When we're in the midst of a battle with temptation, God the Son is *able* to help you. When we are in the throes of shame after giving into sin *yet again*? God the Son is *able* to comfort you. When everything around us, our hopes, our dreams, our desires, our relationships, our family life, our friendships, our grades, whatever it may be? When they're falling apart. God the Son is powerful enough to reach into our weakness. And help us.

We can call out to Jesus and know that He can aid us. Why? Because *he is God*. He isn't simply a super strong hero, like Batman. He's more than a vigilante in a cape. He's God. The author of the book of Hebrews says this:

[Hebrews 1:3b] *He upholds the universe by the Word of His power.*

Christ upholds the *universe*. If he does that, then you know that he can come to you in *your world*. And that means that you can cry out to him in the storms of life. From the hurricanes of sin. From the pits of addiction. From the chains of bitterness. From the grime of lust. From the isolated prison cells of the ivory towers of arrogance and self-righteousness. From whatever pit or quagmire you've found yourself in, you can know that Jesus, God the Son eternal, unique, all-powerful, all-glorious, can reach down into *your* place, *your* despair, *your* brokenness. And comfort *you*.

That should be such an encouragement to you. That there's a God who *does* know your concerns. He hears your prayers and knows your circumstances. He isn't distantly disinterested in your life. He's not a cosmic taxman, demanding a tithe but not particularly bothered about you. He's God the Son, your creator. He created *you*. He knows you *better than you know yourself*. He knows the hairs on your head, the order of your veins, and even knows about *that* birthmark! He knows you intimately because he formed you intentionally. With love and compassion. He created you. And he cares for you.

But if that's *all* Jesus is? God? Well, that's wonderful and amazing – but it means our *fundamental problem* hasn't been fixed. We're unable to access our heavenly Father. Our fundamental problem is larger than our difficulties or trials or even our health. Our biggest problem is that we are sinners. Consider what John says in verse 9 of the same passage:

[John 1:9] *The true Light, which enlightens everyone was coming into the world.*

[10] *He was in the world, and the world was made through Him, yet the world did not know Him.*

[11] *He came to His own, and His own people did not receive Him.*

Do you see what John's saying here?

God the Son, the eternal, majestic, transcendent, glorious God was *rejected* by his creation. He who *made* everything, every*one*, was cursed at, spat upon, and rejected. By his own creation. Why? Because we're sinners. And sin is an electric fence, a boundary, a barrier, a ditch, a chasm that we cannot cross. Because God is *holy* and *good*. But human beings, created beings? By nature, we're wicked and evil.

To be sure, Jesus did not create us that way. But when Adam and Eve sinned in the garden, humanity was enslaved to sin. We became rebels. An illustration I find helpful is this: When Winston Churchill informed England that they were at war with Germany, he meant that the *entire* country was at war. Perhaps some people didn't want to go to war with the Nazis. Nevertheless, because their leader had made the decision, *everyone* else was now at a state of war. This is what happened in the garden of Eden. By resisting God's rule, Adam, the leader of humanity and regent on behalf of God, declared war against his king. And, like the English in World War Two who found themselves at war with Hitler and Germany, all those who are from Adam are now at war with God. Adam sold us out to Satan because we are all *in* Adam, or *from* Adam, or *under* Adam. This rebellion against God, of which we are a willing part, is what the Bible calls sin.

And we, each of us, knows what sin is, instinctively.

The thoughts of our hearts? They are *against* God. We resist God's rules in every area of our lives, don't we? We resist what God says about sex and sexuality, about identity, about lying, about stealing, about respecting authority placed over us, about gluttony or drunkenness. And the list could go on and on and on. We are sinners. We are at war with God. In our nature, our sinful nature, we are enemies of God. Because although Adam declared war on God and we as a race have followed him, it's also true that we're individually guilty of lobbing bombs at God. We lie, we lust, we steal, we slander, we gossip, we commit adultery often in person but certainly in our hearts. We commit idolatry by worshipping other things and other people. Ultimately, we desire to be our own god and, to do that, we must dethrone God in our lives. As Nietzsche summarized it so honestly: "There cannot be a God because if there were one, I could not believe that I was not he." For me to rule over me, I must resist and reject the rule of the creator. Just as John said. He came into the world, but the world didn't know him. Nor, indeed, did even his own people, the covenant people of Israel, know him. Even they rejected Jesus.

We're sinners.

And although God the Son can *help* us in our trials, we're still tainted, defiled, and corrupted by the stench of death and rebellion. Just ask the Old Testament Israelites about the depth and breadth of the problem of sin. Having a nice, pretty, public temple? That didn't fix their problem of sin. For you and for me? Coming to church? That's not enough to fix our *inner* problem of rebellion towards God. We need more than simply a 911 call to fix our *situations*. No. We need more than simply a different circumstance; we need to be fixed. We're *broken*. *We're* the problem. This is what I call the *Mona Lisa Problem*.

The Mona Lisa Problem

You see, we often think we look like this. Who's this? The most famous sorta-smile in all of human history. It's the Mona Lisa by Leonardo Da Vinci. When we think about *ourselves*, we tend to think of ourselves as, fundamentally, good. Pretty. Nice. Holy.

Or, at the very least, good *enough*.

And we often do so by comparing ourselves with other people. Most of us aren't too self-deceived to think we're *perfect*; but we can all point to someone else and say: "But at least I'm not like *her*." I'm basically good enough. Maybe with a *bit* of "attitude." But God and us? Well, we're bros.

But what's the reality? We're sinners. And sin? It dehumanizes us. It makes us *less* like God. Even when we try our best to *look* good and holy? What *God* sees? Is more like Mr. Bean's *Mona Lisa*:

Even with our attempts to *make ourselves* acceptable to God? We only continue to prove our utter inability and weakness to *be* good. And so our innermost humanity, our deepest nature? That is something that is more than just a mistake: It's *sin*! We don't just need a *friend*; we need to be *fixed*. And God knew what we needed.

This is why it's important that we also see that the eternal and creating God the Son *became a human being*. He became truly human. Just as all the attributes of God are found in the divine Word, so too are all the attributes of humanity found in the incarnate Christ. He's not "sort of human" or pretending to be like a human. The incarnate Son is not like Superman who's simply an alien with a (frankly very poor) disguise. No. God the Son *becomes man*.

God **Became Man**

[14] *And the Word became flesh and dwelt among us, and we have seen His glory, glory as of the only Son from the Father, full of grace and truth.*

God Made Flesh: The Incarnation

The Eternal Word, the Son of God becomes flesh. The word for this is "incarnation." That sentence is massive. The divine Son, the eternal Son, the infinite Son, the Son of the Father? He left the throne room of heaven itself. He exchanged robes of light by adding to himself the limits of matter and flesh.

And he became a man. Frail. Weak. With nerve endings that would feel pain. With human impulses that would dictate a routine, such as eating, sleeping, and thirst. With all the ramifications of living within a sinful world.

The Word become flesh.

He would know what it was like to pay taxes. He would work and live in an unjust system. He would feel his muscles tire, experience the sweat of his brow, and yearn for rest. He, the creator who flung the stars into space and painted the aurora borealis? He would know exhaustion.

The Word became flesh.

In terms of biblical allusion, just as verse 1 echoed Genesis, here verse 14 echoes Exodus. The phrase "dwelt among us" means he "tabernacled" among us. In other words, following John's argument from verses 1-3, we now read that the Divine Son, God, *dwelt in the midst* of humanity. This is intentional; John is establishing that God the Son *is* God, and that he came to earth as a human being and dwelt in our midst, just as God had dwelt in the Tabernacle and been present in the midst of His people throughout their wilderness wanderings. God's presence in the midst of his people is a critical part of the storyline of the Bible. God had walked and talked with Adam before the Fall. He had communed with many humans thereafter, including Cain, Noah, Abraham, and Moses. Yet when God's presence was to come to the Israelites? They were terrified and they had told Moses that he should intercede on their behalf

(Exodus 20:18-21). They were too scared to be in God's presence because of his majestic holiness and their innate unholiness. And this was the conundrum that had to be settled. How can human beings, with all of our sinfulness, enter the presence of a most holy God? In Isaiah 6, when Isaiah sees the seraphim and sees the temple of God in the heavenly places, his words *aren't* "praise the Lord, what joy!" No! Isaiah cries out: "Woe is me! For I am lost; for I am a man of unclean lips and I dwell in the midst of a people of unclean lips!" The Israelites understood Isaiah's concern. Sin separates us from God. So how could God restore communion with his creation if we cannot bear the sight of his holiness?

The Word became flesh.

The incarnation does not mean that the Son *gave up* his divinity; it means that he added to his divine nature the frailty, the limitations, the humiliations of material life, such that, in a way, the glory of his divinity and the majesty of his holiness was obscured. Jesus isn't less than God; he's wholly God. But in the incarnation, he's also now truly man. Now, the incarnate Son dwelt amongst his people, not merely in a tented Holy of Holies, but *as one of us*, having taken upon himself human flesh!

And, to make clear that this is not merely some airy-fairy theology, John says that the apostles have *seen* his glory. This glory, in John's Gospel, refers to the work of Christ: His life, death and resurrection. John saw it all. He watched the miracles. He was present at the transfiguration. He wept at the betrayal and crucifixion. He was an eyewitness to the resurrection. He watched with his mouth agape at the ascension. John says he *saw* them. And because he saw them, he and Matthew and Mark and Luke wrote their experiences and recollections down so that we, too, can "see" them.[1]

---

1   Matthew and John were eyewitnesses to these events. Mark, it is commonly accepted, was the amanuensis or scribe for Peter's eyewitness account. As the apostles went from city to city sharing the message of Jesus, it became clear to the early church that they needed to record the words to avoid confusion, distortion,

But think of what this means, friends. God, the infinite, glorious, majestic, all-powerful Son? He took upon himself human flesh and was wrapped in an embryo. He kicked in Mary's womb. His cells grew and spread and developed just like yours. For nine months, the sovereign Son was enclosed in the womb of a young teenage Jewish girl. He was born in due time, and, just like each of us, he was covered in gunk that needed to be cleaned. He was human as we are human, needing the skin-to-skin contact of the embrace of his parents. As an infant he cried for milk. As a toddler he experienced pain and confusion. As a child he walked with friends and laughed. As a teenager he was trained in his father's trade. As a young man, he took on responsibilities for his siblings.

We see the truth of his humanity throughout the gospel accounts. Jesus walked and talked with his disciples every day throughout his ministry. He grew frustrated with them at their inability to grasp his message. That frustration was borne from his love for them; he *wanted* them to get it. He grew hungry. He experienced exhaustion and fell asleep, infamously at the onset of a storm! He was a handyman, trained most likely in carpentry and stonemasonry. He joked with his friends. He cried the despondent cry of grief at the tomb of Lazarus. He felt a sense of fear at the immanence of the cross. In Gethsemane, he understood the biological pain as well as the spiritual suffering he would endure. And it caused him to plead with his Father that the cup of judgement should not fall on him if there was any other way. In all his experiences as a human being, he demonstrated that he was *truly* human. Just like you and me.

or deception. Thus, Mark wrote for Peter and his account would have remained in the newly planted church to remind them and teach them Christ's work and words. Luke's account is slightly different. He appears to be writing to someone named Theophilus (Luke 1:1 and Acts 1:1). Despite not having witnessed the events in his gospel account, Luke writes like an historian, collating information from eyewitness sources amongst Jesus' and the apostles' contemporaries. The fact the various accounts present different angles of the events does not diminish their truthfulness but enhances the sense of reliability. Each onlooker of any event will gravitate towards certain things that impacted or interested them. This is the case in each of our four biographies of Jesus.

But he was *unlike* us in one crucial respect. He never sinned. Even when directly challenged by the master deceiver and the supreme archnemesis in the wilderness, Jesus refused to buckle under the pressure and seductive lies of Satan. He did not sin against his mother and father. He never told a lie. He never rejected the will of God the Father. Even in Gethsemane, when he asked God to remove the cup of wrath from him, he concluded with the obedient "not my will be yours be done." In every aspect of his life, Jesus was truly human; but he was also the True Human: The obedient and holy Adam. He was human like Adam. But he was *greater* than Adam and Abraham and Israel and David and you and me. He was *sinless*.

The Word became flesh. The eternal Son of God became Jesus, Son of Mary.

To provide the antidote to the poison of our sin.

Jesus Take the Wheel

I remember, once many years ago, I was on my way to university in Belfast. It had been snowing. My windscreen was foggy. The sun was at a terrible angle, hitting me right in my eyes, and as I was turning a corner, I careened into the side of a car. Fortunately for all involved, it was a minor accident. The car that I had crashed into, much *less* fortunately for me, was a *Porche*. And so, although that car only needed a single panel replaced…it was not a cheap mistake, I can tell you.

But in that moment, at 19 years old, I had one thing on my mind: Call mum and dad. I didn't know what to do. I'd never been in an accident before. I was surprised, shocked, and annoyed. So of course. I knew who to call for help.

Because we're *sinners*, we are in need of *saving*. And Jesus as *God*? As we discussed above, he can help our *circumstances*, but our problem of sin, our rebellious *nature*, hasn't changed. Just like the Israelites when confronted with the descending Lord to make the covenant, we can't come into the presence of God lest we be consumed by his holiness. Because God is holy, he will not simply ignore our sin. It *must* be dealt with; justice must be served. But if God remains holy and therefore set apart and distant? Then there is no hope for you or I, because we must pay the price of our treason. And that's eternal judgment because we sinned against the eternal God.

In my circumstances on that winter day in Belfast? I could call my parents, and they could calm me down a bit as I panicked at the side of the road. But the accident? It had still happened. The damaged Porsche still needed fixed. Perhaps I was less nervous after talking with them…but I was still very much in the dog's do-do. My situation hadn't changed even if my own demeanor had calmed down. I had a debt to pay for the Porsche. I had to pay the price.

But what happens is incredible. Because what happens is that God the *Son*? He didn't just come along and *comfort* us in our *circumstances*. He came down and *assumed* the *heart of the problem*. He became the *problem of the heart*.

In my case, on that roadside in Belfast? My mum and dad didn't crash. They didn't hit the Porche. They didn't have any part whatsoever in my blame. In my fault. But they said to me: "Don't worry son, *we'll* pay the damage." They stepped *into my* situation, *and they paid* the price. In a *sense*, they *became* the driver of that beaten, old, damaged Hyundai Accent. And they paid to fix the Porche instead of me. (Which was super helpful because I couldn't pay for it.)

And this is what the *incarnation* means for us. As God-made-flesh, Jesus is *able* to step into our mess. Into our problem. Into our shoes. *We* can't fix our problem. Our sin is an infinite chasm. Our sin is a wall much too high to climb. Our sin is a dirtiness much too deep to ever clean off ourselves. We're lost, broken, enslaved, dead in our sin. There's *nothing that we can do*.

But the Word became flesh!

God the Son became Jesus, son of Joseph, God-made-flesh, to step into our world. He stepped into our circumstances. And then, on the cross, he stepped *into our sin*. In fact, he who *knew no sin*? God *made him* to be sin. So that we might become the righteousness of God. This is vital; God the Word couldn't die to save us in his divine nature alone. God is Spirit. He has no flesh. God cannot die. And God cannot be tainted by sin because he is perfect holiness.

But by the addition of *human flesh*? Then Jesus? He can, and did, die *in our place*. Because he is God and man, both sides of the equation are solved and therefore the pattern of salvation is established. Because of Jesus.

As *God* the Son, he was able to bear the *eternal wrath of God that we deserve* for our sinfulness. No man could pay that infinite penalty because we're *finite* and our debt is an infinite debt. But the *infinite* man? He can bear it. And he did bear it. For you and for me.

Because Jesus is truly *human* through the incarnation, he stands as a new Adam. He is a new head of a new humanity. As Jesus, in the likeness of *Adam*? He can stand as a *representative* for humanity. Just as Adam brought sin *into* the world through his covenantal headship? So Jesus brought *redemption* into the world through *his* New Covenant headship.

We need Jesus to be *God* so that *the eternal penalty* for *sinfulness* can be paid.

We need Jesus to be *human* so that *our* eternal penalty for *our* sinfulness can be paid.

Jesus is God. Jesus is man.

And in him we have redemption, the forgiveness of sins.

This is the *glory* of Christmas, of the incarnation, friends. The infinite God became infant man. The infinite became finite. The mighty became meek. The king became a kid. The Lord of all became the lowliest of all. The eternal became temporal. The greatest became as the weakest!

God became man.

And at the cross? The holiest experienced hell. The sinless became the sinner. The innocent became the guilty. The king became the traitor.

But *why?*

Because God Loves You

Christian, this is *vital* for you.
Because Jesus is God, he *can* help you.
Because Jesus became man, he *did* help you.
Because Jesus remains God-made-flesh, he *will* help you.

At the cross, through the incarnation, Jesus didn't just reach down to comfort you in your pits of sin. No, at the cross, *he stepped into them.*

✝ Application: Believe the Gospel

Perhaps you've read this far as someone who still doesn't accept or rest in the gospel of Christ. Maybe someone gave you this little book out of their love for you, or you've picked it up out of mild curiosity? Whatever the reason you've made it this far: Welcome! This is for *you* just as much as it's for me. Jesus became a human being. Just like you and me. But *unlike* you and me he didn't sin. He wasn't in rebellion against God. No, as we've explored, he was God *and* man. And that means He can comfort you in your circumstances. But it *also* means that He can *heal you* from your situation of sin and rebellion.

You know all about sin. You know how it breaks you, humbles you, and controls you. Christ stepped into that. He *became* that. Why? *To free you from it.*

He stepped down into the greasy, sleazy, grime of your sinfulness and mine. He stepped into the grossness of your rude conversations and insults. He stepped into the arrogance of your prideful rebelliousness. He stepped into the hurtfulness of your gossiping and slandering tongues. He stepped into the secrecy of your hiddenmost bitter thoughts. He stepped into the embarrassment of your failures, public and private. He stepped into the pain of your grief and sadness. He stepped into the webs of your deceptions and lies. He stepped into the isolation of your loneliness. He stepped into the poisons of your bitterness. He stepped into the seclusion of your sinful resentments. He stepped into the anxieties that cause you to doubt His goodness.

He stepped into the addictions of your heart. He stepped into the indignity of your pornography use (and a group the size of a regular church gathering, statistically, will have over 70% of men over 30% of women[2] using porn frequently). And pornography actively correlates to sex slavery and trafficking.[3] Christ stepped into even that. He stepped into all your brokenness.

In all your sin. In all your pain, hurt, brokenness, embarrassment, rebellion, resentment? For all your sinful behavior: the lies, the slander, the gossip, the lust, the abuse, the ugly agonies of being sinners in a sinful world? Despite *all* that ghastly grime.

The pure, innocent, holy, spotless, perfect, and gracious Son, eternal, transcendent, majestic, glorious, in his power? He came down to earth. For you. He crawled into the cesspit of our filth and horror and grubbiness. To rescue you from it.

---

2   https://mazeoflove.com/pornography/; https://worldmetrics.org/porn-use-statistics/ The top-ranked pornography site on the web had 700,000,000 more total visits than Amazon and 900,000,000, 1,100,000,000, 1,300,000,000, 1,500,000,000, and 1,800,000,000 more total visits than TikTok, OpenAI, LinkedIn, Netflix, and The Weather Channel, respectively.

3   "The connection to sex trafficking is that increased use of pornography leads to increased demand for prostitution. When demand outstripped supply of local prostitutes, women and children were brought in from overseas, often against their will, Layden told the forum…" ("Online porn addiction turns our kids into victims and predators," *Sydney Sun-Herald*, Aug. 14, 2005 [published at: http://www.smh.com.au/news/miranda-devine/online-porn-addiction-turns-our-kids-into-victims-and-predators/2005/08/13/1123353539758.html]:) "One former porn actress testified, "Women are lured in, coerced and forced to do sex acts they never agreed to do… [and given] drugs and alcohol to help get [them] through hardcore scenes…The porn industry is modern-day slavery." Sex traffickers use pornography in many ways. They force their victims to watch porn to desensitize them. Even to train them in sex acts they will be forced to perform. They also video the victims and sell and distribute the pornographic films on the internet and other outlets." https://cbn.com/news/news/porn-industry-modern-day-slavery-how-pornography-and-sex-trafficking-are-linked

In the incarnation, Christ met you in the pit of your despair. Not simply to give you advice. Not simply to calm you down. Not simply to "sit with you a while." But to *pull you out*. Dear friend, look at the incarnation. Look at God-made-flesh. For you.

And turn your heart to Christ. Repent from your rebellion and become adopted as a child of God. You read in verse 10 that the world didn't know him. In verse 11 you read that his own rejected him. But John didn't conclude his thought there, with rejection:

[12] *But to all who did receive him, who believed in his name, he gave the right to become children of God,*

[13] *who were born, not of blood nor of the will of the flesh nor of the will of man, but of God.*

Right now, you can be born anew, born again, born *of God*. Why wait? Let this moment be the beginning of a new life for you. A life in the family of God.

✝ Application: Rest in Christ

And Christian. Let us be under no illusions that we're sinners. Each and every one of us would never show our face in public again if our thoughts were displayed on a public screen, never mind our texts, our internet usage, our peer-group conversations and so on.

But Christ. He did not count his divinity as something to be grasped at, to keep him *away* from our grubbiness. Instead, he became the incarnate Son, becoming not only a human but a slave (Philippians 2:7) and being obedient even to death on a cross (Philippians 2:9). Because he loved us. Because of his sacrificial death in our place, he has saved us from our sin and he can save us from our false desires. Even from ourselves.

Paul reminds us of this when he dramatically proclaims:

[Romans 8:38] *For I am sure that neither death nor life, nor angels nor rulers, nor things present nor things to come, nor powers,*

[39] *nor height nor depth, nor anything else in all creation, will be able to separate us from the love of God in Christ Jesus our Lord.*

This is shown for us, for you, in that while we were *sinners*, rebels, enemies, wicked, and treacherous, distracted and disinterested, Christ *died* for us. How many kings would do that for you? What about people you know and love and respect? Your pastors? The president or king? What about the teachers or professors, the provost, or the university president from the introduction? I mean. We'll *sit* with you at lunch, sure; but we aren't even willing to sit your *exams* in your place, never mind be responsible for your *soul*.

But *God*. Became *flesh*. For *you*.

How many kings do you know would do this? For you? Let this next Christmas be the first year that you celebrate the hope and joy of the incarnation of Christ for all of its glorious beauty and truth! The Incarnation, the coming of Jesus at Christmastime, tells you that your value, your worth, your dignity, and your identity is *founded* in God, is *grounded* in grace, and thus you are *bound* to *Christ*. Nothing else determines who you are. Not your grades, not your family, not your salary, not your career, not your boyfriend, girlfriend, or spouse. The value God placed on you is such that he did not spare his own Son but sent him to come and to die for you.

God the Son, the pure, radiant, holy Son left the throne room of heaven. And came down to this world. He came into your pit of despair, your quagmire of shame, your grave of grime. And can lift you out of it. What greater truth is there to reflect on than this?

Chapter Two:

...Because of the Crucifixion

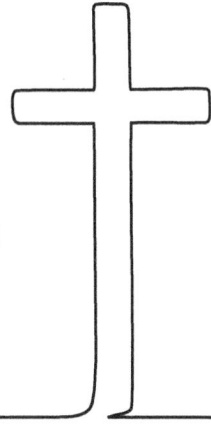

[Luke 23:32] *Two others, who were criminals, were led away to be put to death with Him.*

[33] *And when they came to the place that is called the Skull, there they crucified Him, and the criminals, one on His right and one on His left.*

Introduction

Have you ever felt defeated? Down and out? When I was a kid in what people in the South call elementary school, I was selected to be the goalie (that's the technical term for me being an overweight kid whose duty was to stand on the goal line and try to get hit in the face to stop the opposition from scoring...) for my first ever soccer tournament. It was going to be a round-the-house style tournament, which meant you'd play every opposition team at least once, before the final win-loss ratio would determine if your team had secured enough points to go through to the next round.

It was my first game of my first tournament and I was excited. So much so that I could barely sleep the night before. I remember lying in bed, trying to sleep, holding a tiny soccer ball. It felt like the most important moment of my life. I was raring to go. Excitement coursed through my entire frame as I got my kit on and made my way onto the pitch.

But everything changed in the space of 20 minutes. By 20 minutes we were 4-0 down. Game one. First tournament. Down. Dramatically. I wasn't entirely at fault for all the goals. But I was the last defender. Most significantly for me, however, was that it certainly *felt* like my fault. And our coach? Took me off at 4-0. She replaced me and brought on a substitute. It. Felt. Horrible.

But here's the kicker. Here's what stung more than the embarrassment of losing and of being substituted. The worst feeling in the world was that I realized that I *wasn't* good enough. When Christopher took my place? We actually started to win! And although we didn't win the tournament - not by any means. Not even close. We nevertheless won a game or two. And because Christopher took my place? The entire team, *including* me? We did play better. We got to experience some victory.

But the point? I couldn't do it. I couldn't win it for us. I wasn't good enough.

In this chapter we are going to see that we, each and every one of us, are not good enough. In fact, not only are we *not* good enough, but we're going to see that we've been playing for the *opposite* team. It would be like if my time as goalkeeper had been to intentionally make my team lose.

In this chapter, we will see the fullest, the most gruesome, the most despicable implications of *sin*. We encountered sin briefly in chapter 1, but now we will see what sin truly is and what it desires.

And we will also explore, therefore, what we need in response to the truest reality of sin. Because what we need isn't to *do* better or *be* better. Like my woeful soccer team, we need a *substitute*. We need someone better, something greater, than ourselves. As we walk through Luke 23, we're going to see that God provided that substitute. Someone to take our place. To win the victory we could never win on our own. But to *embrace* that victory? We need to recognize the reality that we're not good enough. That we need God's substitute.

[Luke 23:22] *A third time [Pilate] said to them, "Why, what evil has He done? I have found in Him no guilt deserving death. I will therefore punish and release Him."*

[23] *But they were urgent, demanding with loud cries that he should be crucified. And their voices prevailed.*

[24] *So Pilate decided that their demand should be granted.*

[25] *He released the man who had been thrown into prison for insurrection and murder, for whom they asked, but he delivered Jesus over to their will.*

Jesus Was Condemned By Our Sin

The Context

We jump into Luke's history of Jesus when he has been arrested. By verse 25, Jesus has already been before Pilate, the Roman prelate, once before. Jesus had been sent to Pilate at dawn and Pilate had questioned Jesus then. I suspect Pilate was initially somewhat bemused by the whole situation. After all, he knew the Jewish leaders. Theirs was a somewhat "stormy" relationship, with his cultural mistakes, insults, and downright disregard for the worship of the Jewish God. And now this, this *peasant* from the north had gotten these arrogant priests rattled. He could tell by their accusations that something was amiss.

Pilate had listened to the charge against Jesus. He heard that Jesus claimed to be the *Messiah*. "Whatever that is," he thought. But the Chief Priests interpreted for him: "Pilate, it means *king!*" Perhaps Pilate's ears pricked up at that revelation. He took another look at this shackled man from the north. He didn't dress like any king Pilate had seen. He looked Jesus in the eye, amused, and asked, "*Are* you the king of the Jews?" Jesus' answer, "You have said so" was confident, almost impudent, in its simplicity.

Pilate watched Jesus as he heard the nattering and complaining and accusations from the Chief Priests and elders and scribes. The accusations began to move away from the claims of kingship to other things, and Pilate, still watching Jesus, had motioned for quiet from the Peanut Gallery.

He asked Jesus, "Have you no answer to make? Look at *all* these accusations and charges they're bringing against you!" But, to Pilate's amazement, Jesus remained silent.

In Matthew's gospel, Matthew makes much of this investigation of Jesus' claims by the Roman governor. And this leads us to ask, why does this question of *kingship* matter? It's obvious that the concept of blasphemy didn't really matter to Pontius Pilate. After all, what's one more claimant of divinity in a world of pantheons? Pilate was a Roman and he could not care less that some tribal Jewish god was offended by this rabble rouser from the north.

But a *king* is something different. A king is a threat to a conquering nation. No matter the *legitimacy* of the claims, the very *idea* of a king is dangerous because it reminds a conquered people that they're not free. The fear the priests were trying to stoke in Pilate was the *threat of a rebellion*. Jesus, albeit most likely a scruffy looking, bruised, exhausted, and dirty character by this point, didn't need to *look* like a king. He simply had to *represent* a confidence, an authority, a *potential*, that may present itself as a homegrown alternative to Rome. And there were groups throughout Israel waging guerrilla warfare against the Romans. So, for Pilate, this was a very plausible threat. Thus, after Jesus confirmed the claim of kingship, or at least appeared to do so, his silence remained all the more baffling to Pilate. The accusations continued to fly, but Jesus refused to dignify them with a response. The accusation of 'kingship' nevertheless sat heavily over the court proceedings.

A Davidic King

But what is kingship according to the *Bible*? Well, it's about dominion. It's about authority. But it's *also* about responsibility of that authority. In Eden, Adam, for example, was a small king under the One True King. Adam had authority and dominion and a responsibility both to God and to the creation over which he was given rule. Biblical kingship is an expansive dominion over creation with a divine responsibility and obligation to introduce, cultivate, and exercise God's Law. Though, of course, with the Fall of humanity that status was corrupted and our duty was perverted. Instead we set about breaking God's laws.

Nevertheless, Jesus accepted the title of the "king of the Jews," and so we must understand why this was significant. In 2 Samuel 7, king David was addressed by the prophet Nathan, who told David that God was making a covenant with him. This covenant is for a new king. A greater king. Here's what the Bible says:

[2 Samuel 7:12] *When your days are fulfilled and you lie down with your fathers, I will raise up your offspring after you, who shall come from your body, and I will establish His Kingdom.*

[13] *He shall build a house for my name, and I will establish the throne of His Kingdom forever.*

----

[16] *And your house and your kingdom shall be made sure forever before me. Your throne shall be established forever.*

This promise of a king and a kingdom is extremely significant. It speaks of something infinitely greater than merely the expulsion of Rome. It's an *eternal* kingdom. By that very definition, it *must* require the conquering of death, for death is the enemy of immortality! Thus, by Jesus' acceptance of the title "King of the Jews," he's accepting the scepter from David, as it were. He's acknowledging that he is the fulfilment of the prophetic hopes of the Old Testament.

He's the king that Israel had *waited* for, but he wasn't the king that they *hoped* for. He wasn't going to rule over them immediately. He wasn't going to strike fear into the hearts of Roman legionaries. He wasn't going to overthrow an ever-encroaching Persia. No. He's the Davidic heir, on trial before a Roman governor, at the behest of lying priests. It sounds ludicrous. But, nevertheless, he *is* still the king.

✝ Application: Christ's Kingship

There's a warning here for the Christian. The priests ought to have known better. Pilate? Not so much. He was a pagan, a foreigner, a Roman. But the Jewish priests? They *ought* to have known. And yet they not only didn't recognize their king, but they were actively plotting to kill him. Christian, what does Jesus' kingship mean for you? What does it mean for us, individually? How is Jesus the king over your singleness, for example? How is Jesus the king over your marriage? How is Jesus the king over your family?

Is he?

Or is his kingship, frankly, ignored for the deceptive idea that we are owed a happy, healthy and wealthy life? Such is a Western ideal, sadly, that has become mainstream in watered-down Christian thought. That somehow, simply because I proffer lip service to Christ, I deserve nice things in return: An attractive wife, an attentive husband, and/or a good and functional family (whatever that is).

But Jesus died for far more than simply the American dream. He died that dead men could live! By his death, we are freed to live a life at war with sin, not enslaved by it. By his death, we are freed to love our spouse no matter the depth of injustice and hatred we receive. By his death, we are freed to prayerfully love and enjoy our children, no matter how painfully they hurt us. By his death we are freed to be men and women conformed into his likeness. That means we may not have the perfect wife, or the perfect husband. But it means that *we* can try to *be* the best husband, or the best wife, that we can be, because we can love them with a love that is not merely human, but divine.

Is Jesus the king over our money? Or do we give Jesus the bare minimum, while we enjoy the fruits of our labor. Is our token offering little more than an attempt to "buy Jesus off"? Could we get away with treating our taxes the way we treat investing in the Eternal Kingdom?

Is Jesus the King over our actions? Or do we tell Jesus that *our* sins aren't *that* big of a deal? Especially when we compare them with the local Joe Bloggs of badness?

Is Jesus the King over your church? Or do we feel that, since Jesus isn't doing a good enough job leading, protecting, loving, guarding the church, that we need to become vigilantes? Defending ourselves against being vulnerable, against loving the sinner, against forgiving one another?

Christian, if Jesus *is* king, then he decides the terms for everything. We don't get to decide the terms of our commitment. If he is the king God promised, then we offer him ultimate, complete and utter submission in *all* things!

Jesus' kingship is contrary to the American dream. It isn't about me, me, me, but about him, him, him and then you, you, you. It's about sacrifice for the Kingdom of God. It's about sacrifice for the glory of Christ and the advance of the gospel. It means saying: "I refuse to gossip about you because I love you. I refuse to fight with you because I love you. I refuse to hurt you because I love you. I refuse my rights over yours because I love you." It means saying: "I will stand beside you, because I love you. I'll help you, because I love you. I'll honor you, because I love you. I'll pray for you, because I love you."

It means saying: "I'll sacrifice my pleasure, my dignity, my "face" so that you can see me for who I am." It means that I will ask for your help when I need it. I'll ask for your knowledge when I am lacking. I'll ask for your love when I am unlovable. I'll ask for your forgiveness when I sin against you. I'll ask for your forbearance when I am difficult. Because Jesus is king, and he expects this of me. This is what a church under the kingship of Jesus looks like. It may not be glamorous, but, by God's grace it is *glorious*.

Jesus was asked, "Are you the king of the *Jews*?"

We are asked, "Is Jesus the king of the *me*?" How do you answer that question?

Standing Before Pilate

Let's return to the courtroom.

The Chief Priests had told Pilate that Jesus was a national threat to Rome because he claimed to be King of Israel and had been telling the Israelites to stop paying taxes to the Romans. This was a lie, of course, for we all know the infamous phrase "render unto Caesar that which is Caesar's and to God that which is God's" (Matthew 22:21). Unwilling to be the cause of tension, and quite possibly eager to annoy the Chief Priests, Pilate refused to judge Jesus guilty or innocent but found a technical loophole that allowed him to ship Jesus off to Herod Antipas, the Roman-supported client king over what remained of "independent" Israel. He could do this because Jesus was a Galilean and Galilee was technically part of Herod's jurisdiction.

And when Jesus, in chains, arrived at Herod's throne? Surprisingly, Herod was *thrilled*. Why? What could make Herod *happy* at this 'usurper king of Israel' standing before him? Well, he'd heard about Jesus, hadn't he? And Herod looked at this ragged, chained, wizardy, magic man from the north with childlike anticipation. And demanded: "Perform, puppet. Do the things. Do the signs. Perform for me!" Jesus looked so beleaguered and out of place in the princely palace that Herod didn't feel at all threatened by Jesus; instead, he wanted to be *entertained* by him.

But Jesus? We read in verse 9 that he remained silent. And this makes sense, right? What kind of a king would Jesus be if he was compelled, ordered, forced, to perform like a circus animal? What kind of a king would give in to Herod Antipas, who was cruel, rude, violent, and only propped up in his position of power by the hated Romans?

Jesus said nothing.

And Herod grew bored.

✝ Application: How do you Consider Jesus?

I wonder what you've heard about Jesus? What made you read this chapter today? What do you know of the real Jesus?

There are people out there, in the world, on fancy TV shows and who write bestselling books, and they tell you that Jesus? Well *maybe* he was a real person. But if so, he was little more than a Communist Revolutionary. "But," they say with a sad shake of the head, "in reality he probably didn't even exist."

Then there are people out there wearing ornate academic gowns who teach in universities and colleges. And they tell you that Jesus? Well what matters is his *ideas*. They teach us that it's important to be a good person, to be moral, and strive to be a generally nice and kind human being in our global community. Jesus, they exclaim, was an incredible role model for us to live life well and to stand up for the oppressed and be a defender of the weak. But that's the limit of their engagement with Jesus.

Then there are the people who stand on platforms and show off their bling. And they bear titles like bishop and apostle and pastor. And they tell you that Jesus *wants* you to be happy, healthy, and wealthy. Right here, right now. And the *only* thing keeping that from happening? Is *you*. Your lack of faith is what is hindering God from blessing you.

If you're sick? It's your fault.
If you're poor? It's your fault.
If you're unhappy? It's your fault.
If your job isn't satisfying? That's your fault, too.

Oh! But if you donate to their ministry *right now*, if you trust those self-described magic men and women? Then you, too, can be happy, healthy, wealthy, and wise. Just like they are. And, in case you doubt them? They invite you to look at their expensive watch or necklace with envy. They'll let you see pictures of their multi-million dollar mansions and private jets and say here's the proof! And it can be yours. *If* you give them some money right now. Plant that seed of faith and watch it blossom. Of course, if it *doesn't*? Well. *You* didn't have enough faith, did you?

What Jesus have you heard about?

Herod wanted a court jester, a magician who'd entertain him for a few hours. What Jesus do you want? A genie in a bottle, to give you what you want? A psychiatrist, to listen to your problems? A revolutionary, to stick it to the man? A friend, to make you *feel good* about your decisions? A life-coach, to help you *make* good decisions?

How about the Jesus of Luke 23? A prisoner standing silent before a peacocking king? Seemingly frail. Apparently so pathetic he couldn't even speak. Let me encourage you. Look at *this* Jesus. Because although it *looks* like the game is over. And He *appears* weak and pathetic and defeated?

It's *this* Jesus, *this* king, that truly matters.

Back to Pilate

Unsurprisingly, Herod grew bored with the silent Jesus. After it was clear to him that Jesus wasn't going to be a performing monkey, he sent him back to Pilate. Herod was politically crafty enough to know that it would be injudicious to kill Jesus for pretending to be a king. After all, he just had to look at Jesus to see he was little more than a ragamuffin peasant from the north. There was no real threat to Herod's political power. Not so long as he had Roman favor. It would only hurt his already disastrous poll ratings with the Israelites to kill Jesus who was, by his calculations, harmless to him. No, thought Herod. It's better that it's Pilate's problem. So off Jesus was marched once again, back across the city, to Pilate's house.

Before we go any further, let's take a moment to consider this pivotal character in the narrative: Pontius Pilate. We know from all the gospel accounts that Pilate was not terribly eager to condemn Jesus as an innocent man. And you may have heard before that Pilate was, therefore, a coward because he refused to protect this innocent man from this horrendous injustice. But I want to dispute that. I don't think Pilot was a coward. Rather, I think he was a cold, calculating, and pragmatic leader. Listen to how the Jewish historian Philo speaks of Pilate:

> *He was a spiteful and angry person...He feared that if they [the Jews] really sent an embassy [to the Emperor], they would...specify in detail his venality, his violence, his thefts, his assaults, his abusive behavior, his frequent executions of untried prisoners, and his endless savage ferocity.*[4]

Although Philo is a biased historian (he's Jewish), the point seems unavoidable that Pilate was not a fair or just leader, but neither was he afraid of shedding innocent blood. Thus, in his condemnation of Jesus he wasn't *afraid* of the crowd. I rather suspect he wanted to annoy the Chief Priests by trying to free Jesus. It's also possible that, at Passover, the risk of a riot would make him look bad to his Emperor. And that was something he was eager to avoid. This is why Pilate tried to use the annual tradition whereby every Passover he would pardon a criminal. It's a piece of pageantry akin to the President of the United States pardoning a turkey each thanksgiving. Pilate tried to get Jesus "off the hook" by offering to the people a clear choice: A popular, yet evidently ineffective, rabble-rouser, Jesus, or a known, violent terrorist in Barabbas.

Upon hearing this horrendous turn of events and fearing that even now Jesus may slip through their fingers, the leaders scrambled and took control of the crowd. They began to turn it into a mob, baying for blood. Granted, Pilate tried to reason with the crowd, asking, "Well, what shall I do with this king of the Jews?" But the crowd, having been whipped into their frenzy, responded with the chilling demand: "Crucify him." Again, Pilate tried to avoid condemning Jesus to death: "But why? What evil has he committed?" Yet the crowd, unwilling to be reasoned with, merely shouted all the louder: "Crucify him!"

Can you see the evil that has incentivized this scene?

---

4   Philo, *Embassy to Gaius*, XXXVIII:302.

Jesus had been *denied* by Peter.

He'd been *lied about* by the Chief Priests.

He'd been *derided* by Herod.

He'd been *pragmatized* by Pilate.

Now he's being *decried* by the crowd.

This should be a very strong warning to us, shouldn't it? We must be so careful to differentiate between the culture of the world around us and the culture of the kingdom that Christ has inaugurated. Otherwise, we simply become like the Chief Priests – warriors for the wrong cause. How often, in church history, have we seen this happen? How often, in local churches, have we heard of this happening?

We must beware, and indeed confront, the voices in the culture who tell us that Jesus primarily wants us to be happy, healthy and wealthy. We must confront the voices that tell us that God cannot be a God of justice because of a, b, or c reasons. We must confront the voices that tell us that certain people are above reproach and rebuke. We must confront the voices that tell us that certain sins are okay, now, because we understand more than the inspired authors of Scripture.

But it doesn't stop at the culture *out there*, does it, friends? We must be extremely careful to see the log in our own eyes. We must be careful, lest we find ourselves *preaching* Christ, but *living* our own theatrical politics. There is a danger in so closely identifying politics with Jesus because the kingdom of God is bigger than our earthly political preferences.

We must be careful, lest we get so caught up in the beautiful ideals of *changing* culture, that we begin to be *conformed* to culture by reverse-engineering. We don't offer simply a *social* gospel, we offer the *eternal* Gospel. And yes, it *can* change society, but *only* after Christ has changed the heart.

We must be careful, lest we allow the temporary allure of earthly power to sidetrack our *global* mission of love, mercy, compassion and proclamation. We are to love the orphan, not merely the fetus. We are to love the terrorist, not merely the cultural reflection.

And all of this is because of what we see here. If we learn one thing, let it be this: The enemy will *never* compromise. If he orchestrated the death of the king, what makes us think that he will be any less merciless and methodical with us?

If he can't destroy us, he'll deceive us.
If he can't deceive us, he'll distract us.
If he can't distract us, he'll delight us.

All the while, we'll become ineffective for the Kingdom, and we'll bring dishonor on our king.

This is why church is so important. We need one another to help us along the way. I need you. And you need me. Because we both have blind spots. We both have weaknesses. And we both have strengths. We can help each other. So that when the moment comes, and we're being challenged to deny our king, we will have the strength and the support to be counted with him, no matter the cost.

Pilate Decides...

Pilate was surprised that Jesus was returned to him. It was even more surprising to see that Jesus was now wearing fancy clothes too. Herod had mocked Jesus by dressing the prisoner like a king. This kind of wry, dark humor appealed to Pilate and this action actually helped broach a rapprochement between the two leaders.

But Pilate's political problem had boomeranged back to him. The Chief Priests were adamant that Jesus was to be punished by Rome. "Punished" in their mind meant executed. But Pilate knew that he was on thin ice with the emperor. He'd already caused a riot once before and that had, it seems, led to an official rebuke. Publicly executing a peasant from the north who had a large following would inflame the crowds who had gathered to celebrate Passover and possibly lead to a riot. As the quotation from Philo attests,

Pilate sought to avoid giving the Emperor any reason to think of him as incompetent or inept. Thus, Pilate tried to privately deflate the situation.

"Jesus," he said, "is innocent of any crime. Therefore, I'll simply punish him and free him."

But the priests were insistent. And they riled up the crowd. And the crowd demanded that Jesus be crucified. And Pilate? Withered. The energy and demands of the crowd were loud. And Pilate feared a riot. This was Passover. Passover is the holiest of holidays in the Jewish calendar; that means that it was busy. Jerusalem's population had grown to nearly a million people. A riot could become a full-blown rebellion.

And so Pilate makes a cold political calculation: "Well," he reasons, "It's better that one man die than a rebellion breaks out."

"Fine," Pilate says. "Release Barabbas. The terrorist. The robber. The insurrectionist. Release him. This Jesus, your king? Your Messiah? I hand him over to you." Jesus, we see in Luke 23:25, was "delivered over to their will."

Think of that phrase for a minute. Jesus, who had healed so many Israelites, who had taught them the heart of Scripture, who was their Messiah, who came and lived in their midst as God-made-flesh was delivered "over to their will." And what was their will?

Not to enthrone him.
Not to embrace him.
Not to honor him.

Jesus was delivered over to his own people who desired to devour him. They demanded to destroy him. They wanted to *crucify* him.

✝ Application: The Heart of Sin

There's been a cosmic battle raging from before the dawn of time. We want to be careful not to make it appear that there are two equally powerful opposing forces. That's a heresy called dualism, that Good and Evil, or Ying and Yang, or whatever you want to call it, are constantly fighting, and eventually, hopefully, good will win out. We aren't talking about *that*. Yet, nevertheless, Scripture is indeed clear that, although God remains sovereign even over the very fact and action of evil, there is indeed an ongoing cosmic rebellion.

It began in the heavens with Lucifer, once an angel of glory, given access to the throne of heaven and to God himself. But Satan, rather than worship God, decided to mount a coup. Lucifer wanted to *be* God. And he rebelled. But, of course, it failed. Thus, Lucifer was cast out.

In due course he made his way to little planet earth, where God had carefully created a people who reflected his very character, with their given ability to choose or refuse obedience. They had free will, just like the angels. And this fallen angel encouraged Eve, one of God's human beings, to distrust God, and instead trust herself. Deceived, she chose to eat the fruit of disobedience and disobey the commands of God. She then encouraged Adam, her husband, to do likewise. And in that act of rebellion, all of creation, all of humanity, was now embroiled in the cosmic coup.

But God *is* the king. And rebellion has consequences. What were the consequences of humanity's rebellion and disobedience? Death. Yet even in that moment, when humanity chose to rebel? God chose to provide grace. He not only refused to kill his rebellious creatures immediately, despite their treachery, but he also promised that someday, sometime, in the future, there would be *restoration*.

But for now, the relationship between God and man would be severed. There would be enmity between man and woman. There would be conflict between good and evil. There would be violence between siblings. Sin would reign. And evil would run rampage throughout the created order.

Adam and Eve, too, were cast out from the presence of God. They were exiled from the garden. And the very next generation, their son, committed murder.

Today, millennia later, we still see the results of this cosmic rebellion. Sexual exploitation is merely a marketing technique.

Corruption and greed are signs of success. Violence is paid for and celebrated. Murder is a medical procedure. Unconstrained lust is a right. Science is king.

And God, we hear, is dead, and we have killed him, as the saying goes.

This is the heart of our sin, isn't it? To be like Satan in the heavens and to be like Adam and Eve in the garden of Eden. To dethrone God. To deny him. To destroy him. In Genesis 4 we read that sin crouches at the door, desiring to dominate us. In 1 Peter 5 we're reminded that Satan is prowling around like a roaring lion seeking whomever he can devour.

But here in Luke 23? Sin, and Satan, was nipping at the heels of Jesus himself. Like a trained hunter, Satan was stalking his ultimate prey and was using his willing vassals, his unthinking human slaves, even (especially!) the *religious* ones! Oh, what a delicious irony that would have been for him.

This is sin. This is the heart and soul and will of sin. Sin seeks to kill, to destroy, to ruin, to hurt, to defeat, to humiliate its captive.

I hope you reflect a little on this. Because in your own lives, I know you know this. I certainly know this experience.

When we lie, we betray ourselves and others. We consider them unworthy of truth. When we lust, we dehumanize those around us and see them only as objects to be used and/or abused. When we lash out in anger, we rob those around us of dignity and value, turning them into punching bags for our gratification. When we steal, we take not only someone's stuff, but we take their trust and we spit on it.

And sin? It's worse than that. Because the ultimate consequence of sin is that it *kills*. Our relationships suffer, don't they? Our friendships struggle. Our marriages weaken when the foxes of sin start running amok.

But those are all *symptoms* of the disease of sin.

But *grasp* the *heart* of sin. Sin looks at God and it stares the Son of God directly in his face and says: "I want you to die." I want to be the king of my own life. I want to reign. And if I'm going to reign? Then, you, God, must die.

Pilate? He gave Jesus over to their will. And what was their will? To take Jesus over into the barracks. Spit on his face. Punch him. Mock him. Beat him into a pulp. Tie him to a pole and whip him bloody. This scourging is a very horrific thing. We tend to get caught up in the action at the cross, and we can skip past this. But the traditional scourging was done by Roman soldiers who were strong men, violent-natured, and didn't like those they conquered. They used a metal-tipped rope, sometimes with a number of flays, that stuck into the skin as they lashed you, and then when they pulled back, they ripped the skin off the back. This was horrifically violent and in and of itself could often be fatal.

This is what *we* want to do and what *every single sin* symbolizes. Unless we are redeemed by Christ, we are actively in rebellion against Christ.

Pilate, however, attempted to wash his hands of it. I don't think this exonerates him; rather, because of his weakness, he was simply saying: I don't agree with you, but I'm going to let it happen. In a way, it makes his decision even more despicable. But even more execrable is that the crowd *loved* to claim it for themselves: "Yes," they cried. "His blood will be on us and our children." Now this is *not* saying that *all Israelites* are guilty and bear a curse. After all, the disciples were Israelites. But it *does* remind us that all who love their sin? That this is what it means: To bathe in the blood of the Son of God.

And so the crowd got their way. The Priests had their execution. Pilate had his peace. Everyone was content. But justice was not done. Pilate handed Jesus over to the Roman soldiers who oversaw executions, and they led him into the palace where they mocked him.

As a military unit, they humiliated and insulted this *king* by dressing him in the color of royalty. They gave him a faux coronation with a crown made from thorns, piercing his scalp and forehead. They saluted him in the Roman manner, mocking him, offering him false worship and homage. They continued to beat him with their fists and spit on him. All of this was part of the pageantry. Part of the humiliation. Part of the execution.

Remember, Jesus had already been whipped. The purple cloak would have caked to the wounds in his back as his blood dried. Blood dripped off his back and arms. Weakened by the loss of blood and repetitive punches, he would have stumbled with each renewed attack. And yet, from bloodshot eyes, looking at out the mocking battalion of soldiers, the King of Kings refused to react with violence: He did not strike out. Like a lamb to the slaughter, he courageously accepted each and every indignity, because his love far surpassed their hatred and their violence.

But *their* behavior reflects *our* hearts. We are each of us God-killers. This means that Jesus? Was condemned by *our* sin. Because we wanted him dead. And where was God in all of this? God *let* Jesus be delivered over to our will. This was not cosmic child abuse, however. God the Son had willed himself to come. There's no division or disunity within the Godhead. Even at Gethsemane, when the humanity of Jesus was faced with the realization of the torture he would endure? Even then, Jesus still said that the Father's will was right and the incarnate Christ would obey. Because he, too, wanted to be our substitute.

✞ Application: Love like Christ

Beloved Christian, keep your eyes focused on Jesus. This, *this*, is what real love looks like. It isn't about your rights, or mine. It isn't about getting what we want, or what we feel we deserve. Divine love is sacrificial. Jesus, despite the injustice, indignity and violence of this moment, refused to defend himself. He refused to call upon the armies of heaven, who, no doubt were standing by. And instead, he looked upon the humans that he had created, yet who were now gleefully preparing to murder him, with love.

Christian. When we read in Scripture that we're to love one another, it's *this* type of love that we're to exhibit. A love that loves unconditionally, because we've been loved first, with perfect love. And because we have the Spirit of this king residing within us, we *can* love sacrificially. We *must* love in this way.

This is a scene that's horrendously gory; but it's a scene wrapped in glory. Culture, and the world as we saw, will never compromise. But look at the king! *He'll* never be defeated. His power, his might, his authority is never in question. His silence isn't cowardice; it's courage. His submission isn't defeat; it's deliberate. His death isn't the end; it's a beginning.

And Christian, with every blow that stuck his head. With every whip that tore flesh from his back. With every curse that hit his face. With every spit that rolled down his cheek. With every kick that made him stumble. With every indignity he faced, *he stood in our stead.*

All that *he* took, and endured, *we* deserved. And it's *because* of Jesus that we don't have to face such judgement. Yes, the world may attack us now, temporarily. But he's taken more than we will ever be faced with, as we will see below. And we can have the confidence that, although he's mocked in this scene with irony, and cruel intent, his actions ensured that we are able to worship him as he deserves.

But after this degradation, and when he was bloodied and weakened to the point of exhaustion, they dressed him in his clothes again and led him out towards Golgotha.

To kill him.

Is this the end, we might ask? Has God thrown in the towel? Has Satan won? Has the coup *finally* triumphed? Absolutely not!

Jesus Was Crucified For Our Sin

[Luke 23:32] *Two others, who were criminals, were led away to be put to death with Him.*

[33] *And when they came to the place that is called The Skull, there they crucified Him, and the criminals, one on His right and one on His left.*

The Crucifixion

After Jesus was beaten to a bloody pulp, abused and mocked, they determined that he was to carry the crossbeam of the cross. He would carry the implement of his own execution to the place of his murder. The soldiers brought Jesus out of the Praetorium, or Pilate's military compound. And as he left the palace, a soldier came to him, kicked him to his knees and grabbed his arms. They took some rope, and tied the crossbeam to his arms, over his shoulders. He was then hoisted to his feet and the soldiers pushed him forward.

"March, king," they mocked.

A week prior, Jesus had had an anticlimactic entrance into the city, riding on a donkey. Yes, it was a surreal experience; but the crowds had rejoiced. They'd thrown palm leaves before his little donkey and cried: "Hosanna!"

Oh, how the crowd had changed since then. Here, in yet another public march, an ironic, humiliating, macabre version of a Roman Triumph, the king was made to trudge through the narrow streets carrying his own cross. No longer did he hear: "Hosanna" but "crucify him" and "death to the traitor!"

Weakened by blood loss, aching from the gaping wounds, the crossbeam on his shoulders weighed him down, he staggered. His tormentors punched him and yelled at him: "March, 'king!'"

But he could not. With the fatigue from the violence he had received, combined with the hunger and thirst of his body, he was unable to keep going. He managed only to make it to the gate of the city where the Roman soldiers grabbed a bystander, Simon from Cyrene. (Talk about being in the wrong place at the wrong time.) The Romans forced Simon to carry the cross of this condemned man.

Jesus limped and stumbled through the streets, up the hill, to the Place of the Skull: Golgotha. Calvary. Every step was agony. Every breath was labored. Every movement weakened him further. Every moment was torture.

And he endured all of it for you and for me.

When they arrived, as they prepared the execution, they offered Jesus some wine with gall, or myrrh, as Mark's account tells us. It's often been taught that this was an act of mercy by the soldiers, given to this poor, wretched man about to die. Some suggest that these soldiers wanted to administer a narcotic to numb the pain.

Unfortunately, that's highly unlikely. Myrrh doesn't act as a pain reliever. Instead, when mixed with wine, the drink would become almost unswallowable. It would have become extraordinarily bitter; and, on Jesus' blood-cracked lips and dehydrated tongue, it would have stung as well as tasted revolting. This act of supposed mercy was another indignity, another torment, another humiliation.

"Here, *Messiah*," they mocked. "Drink this." He tasted it, and it was vile, and he spat it out. The myrrh, as Mark tells us, was the content; Matthew describes its taste: Gall. Like bitter poison.

But there *is* something theological about all this. Matthew uses "gall" to teach us about Jesus' work. King David penned a Psalm titled "Save Me O God." In this Psalm, David was prophetically pointing towards the Greater David, the Messiah. He wrote this:

[Psalm 69:20] *Reproaches have broken my heart, so that I am in despair. I look for pity, but there was none, and for comforters, but I found none.*

[21] *They gave me poison for food, and for my thirst they gave me sour wine to drink.*

In this Psalm, David concluded by saying that God will redeem his people and restore them. But David wouldn't, didn't, couldn't have known just *how* God would bring the restoration.

It would come through David's own future descendant, Jesus, who, unlike David, would be forced to experience all the torture and humiliation without *any* respite. Or break. Or mercy. Where David in his Psalm explained that he was delivered *from* his enemies? Jesus was delivered *to* his enemies. And they, in turn, delivered him to death.

Remember, no one at this scene respected Jesus. To the Romans, he was just another traitor. To the Jewish leaders, he was an arrogant, dangerous upstart getting what he deserves. To the onlookers, he was a blaspheming failure.

✞ Application: The Shame of the Cross

After Jesus spat out the bitter gall, they stripped him. For a Jew, this was extremely shameful and humiliating. There's significantly more to this insult than we understand today. The *shame* of the cross is so often overlooked or underrepresented as part of the torment.

Most of us, I suspect, struggle with guilt. We feel and experience guilt for our actions and our thoughts. But many of us also experience the weight of *shame*. And this is significantly more difficult for us to identify and express. Yet look at Jesus. He understands you when you're feeling ashamed. He understands that feeling acutely. Whether it's the shame of sexual sin, or the shame of pornography use, or the shame of feeling weak, or the shame of abuse, or the shame of failure, or the shame of being caught in sin, or the shame of your past that you can't shake? Whatever shame it is, Jesus understands.

And he was *made* shameful so that you can be free from shame. In the shame of the cross, he bore *your* shame. You don't need to continue feeling and living with that shame, just like you don't need to continue living under the slavery of sin, you don't need to lower your eyes in shame. You don't need to hide yourself from others. Shame is no longer your identity. Christ has set you free. You are *free* in him. Repent of the sin and live in the freedom that he *has* won for you.

The Death of the King

On Calvary's hill, they forced Jesus onto the main beam, which would be the vertical beam when it is erected. They then took one arm and held it against the crossbeam. And a thick, long iron nail was placed on his wrist. And hammered through. Then the other side. Both were moments of sharp, excruciating pain. Next, they placed his feet on the footplate. And another nail mercilessly hammered through. More agony coursed through every sinew of his being, and he hoarsely cried out, gasping at the severity of the pain. His body contorted by the torture, but he couldn't even roll into the fetal position. These battle-hardened soldiers, these professional executioners? They didn't flinch at his cries. They didn't care. Why would they? It was simply another day at the office for them.

Then the soldiers grabbed the ropes and pulled; the cross was raised up and gravity began its work. In order to take a breath, Jesus would have to raise himself up by placing his weight on his feet and pulling on his arms, pulling against the nails that held his frame in place. When he had gulped in a breath, his arms would relax and his legs would give out and he would jolt back down, his flesh yanking against the nails. For every labored breath, gravity would cause more pain, more trauma, and more suffering.

Think of the cruel irony of it. The author of creation. The Word by whom all things were created. The architect of everything. Was suffocating by his own creation of gravity. He was being held to a cross by elements he had formed. And as gravity acted on him, his lungs contracted and expanded as he raised himself to breathe. Slowly, he lost energy. He would continue to weaken and tire. Remember, he hadn't slept the previous night, having been shunted back and forth from various kangaroo trials. And, with blood loss, hunger, and thirst, all taking their toll, his organs began shutting down. His body would enter systemic shock. And he would slowly die.

Then, to make matters worse, they took his clothes, even still covered with his dried blood, and began to gamble for them, to see how they'd divide the spoils. If ever there was a scene where a man looked completely devoid of dignity and purpose, surely this must be it?

Beaten, bloodied, nailed to a cross, his own clothes gambled over beneath him while he suffered and cried out in agony. Yet, even here, the king remained in control. It may not look like it, but we see the evidence in Psalm 22. Another of the Messianic Psalms, verse 18 shows us that God had *planned* this event even down to the smallest details, so that we would know that Jesus' death was not an accident nor a mistake.

Just like the bitter gall, and now, just like the gambling over his clothes, we see that God had ordained the rejection of the king as well as the execution of the king:

[Psalm 22:16] *For dogs encompass me; a company of evildoers encircles me; they have pierced my hands and feet –*

[17] *I can count all my bones – they stare and gloat over me;*

[18] *they divide my garments among them and for my clothing they cast lots.*

Do you see? This was *not* outside God's plan. The Triune God ordained the piercing of Jesus. God foresaw even the gambling over Jesus' clothes. Even in this, the humiliation, Jesus the king remained in control.

But the onlookers didn't make this connection when they read the title that had been hammered onto the cross: "The king of the Jews." It was written not to *identify* Jesus, but to explain his *crime*. It was an attempt to discredit his kingship as well as irritate the Chief Priests. Pilate's cruel capriciousness was to knowingly kill an innocent man. But on the cross, Pilate reminded the Chief Priests that *they* were indeed *not* free. They may have rejected this king from Galilee, but Pilate was reminding them that *they* had no king but Caesar. And this charge claimed that Jesus was guilty of treachery against Rome (rather than blasphemy for which the priests had wanted him dead). But this is greater than simply treachery.

The Mockery of the King

He *was* the king of the Jews. And it was *they* who were the traitors. Jesus was *executed* by Gentiles. But He was *rejected* by his own people. This was cosmic treason. Deicide! God, made flesh, killed in the flesh by his own creation.

Pain was shooting through his body, from the thorns in his head, to the wounds on his back, to the nails in his hands and feet. His dignity was in tatters: He was naked, bloody, beaten, bruised, weak, and dehydrated. And those who passed by looked at him. They looked at this sorry excuse for what remained of a human being, and they *laughed* at him. They threw his words in his face, mocking his claims that "he would rebuild the temple in three days!"

"Why," they jeered, "He can't even get off the cross. So much for destroying the temple!"

Then the Chief Priests, yet further incriminating themselves as the wicked shepherds prophesied by Ezekiel, continue to mock him, saying: "He cannot save himself, yet he saved others!" These religious leaders, who should at the very least have been horrified at the death of an innocent citizen, instead refused him even that, and continued to rebel against their Messiah as they cruelly mocked him.

I wonder, do you grasp just *how* despicable this is? To condemn Jesus is bad enough. But here they were, attending his execution simply to mock him further. This is so much crueler. And it reveals the depths of the wickedness of *their* hearts, doesn't it?

And they mocked him and said: "Oh, if you're *really* the Messiah of God? Then get down. *Then* we'll worship you." Does that language sound familiar?

Remember when Jesus was taken out to the wilderness for his temptations in Matthew 3? What did Satan say?

"Jesus, if you *are* the Son of God? Then turn the stones into bread."

Now, here, that insidious serpent had returned in the voice of these priests: "Oh, but Jesus. Just come down. If you're *really* the Son of God, then wouldn't God want you to avoid suffering? If you're really eager to have a kingdom? Then do something dramatic; come *off* the cross and these Israelites will make you their king. They will!" Even at this moment, Satan was tempting Jesus to denounce the mission of the Messiah and to reject the strategy of God.

But Jesus ignored their wicked taunts.

And yet the accusations of the Chief Priests are so misinformed, aren't they? Rather than Jesus being *unable* to save himself, he voluntarily remained upon the cross. Because if he *saved himself,* he wouldn't have been able to *save us*. Therefore, it wasn't the case that he *could not* save himself. Rather, because of his infinite love and trust in his Father, he *would not* save himself. This is the king that we worship. They should have known better, but these religious leaders have shown their carnality and viciousness.

And still their mockery continued. You can hear them *spit* the words out, with venom: "Let the *Christ*, the *king* of Israel, come down now from the cross, that we may see and believe." Shame on them. They bathed in the blood of their Messiah.

And yet, if we understand sin correctly, *everyone* is guilty of this violence, right? Gentiles cruelly torturing him. Jews cruelly mocking him. The Chief Priests and elders and leaders guilty of conspiring in the kangaroo court against him. Pilate, the governor representing Caesar, pragmatically killing an innocent man. My sin and yours placing him there. Everyone is guilty.

Except the one man, hanging, bloody, bruised, beaten, abused, and abased.

He alone was innocent.

But dying for the guilt of mankind. The answer to Adam's rebellion. The scapegoat. The sacrificial lamb. The true Temple. The greater David. Forsaken by all.

And *still* it gets worse. For not only do the passers-by and the religious leaders mock him. But even other *criminals*, hanging from crosses next to him, mock him. Even they revile him. There are *no* comforting voices recorded in Mark's account. He's blasphemed. He's mocked. He's reviled by his own people. He's rejected by all. From the closest of his disciples, to the empire of Rome, to the religious leaders, to the criminals dying beside him.

All brutally rejected him.

But what was most terrifying of all? Is that this was still only the *earthly* violence. This was the rebellion of man. This was what *we* want to do to God. We haven't even considered what *God's* holiness wants to do to *our* wickedness.

Yet this is horrendous enough, isn't it? If only that were all he endured. But, alas, there's more.

The Judgement of the King

Jesus was crucified. As we can see from Luke 23:39, a synonym for crucifixion is "hanging from a tree." In Deuteronomy 21, we see the full weight of what's happening at that moment:

[22] *"And if a man has committed a crime punishable by death and he is put to death, and you hang him on a tree,*

[23] *his body shall not remain all night on the tree, but you shall bury him the same day, for a hanged man is cursed by God.*

What does this tell us? Theologically, sin is more than anti-God. We've already seen that sin wants to kill God. When Jesus, who is God the Son, was delivered over to humanity, we crucified him. Sin kills God. But now we see the *other* side of the equation.

Jesus? He is God-made-flesh. He *allowed* himself to be handed over *so that* he could bear the curse. But *what* curse? Well, if we flick back a little further from Deuteronomy to Genesis 3, we see the beginning of humanity's enslavement to sin. There humanity's first sin led to punishment. And what does God say to Adam in verse 19?

By the sweat of your face you shall eat bread, till you return to the ground, for out of it you were taken; for you are dust, and to dust you shall return."

Death is the *curse* of God *for* sin. To *sin* is to seek to kill God. But *to be a sinner* is to be under the penalty of death. It is to sit under the righteous condemnation of God. Sin brings God's judgment. Because sin makes us guilty. And Paul tells in Romans 6:23 that the "wages of our sin" is death. We have literally *earned* death *because* we're sinners. But see here, on the cross? The sinless Jesus gave himself over to wicked rebels to be crucified *for* our sin. But he was bearing the judgement *of* sin *from* God that we deserved.

As the king was hanging from the cross, his broken body racked with pain, an eerie, unnatural darkness had fallen over the land.

This tells us that nature itself was mourning the wicked scene of man's cavorting in the blood of God. Creation itself was horrified at what humanity was doing. It's as if creation itself was trying to hide our shameful behavior.

All the way back in Genesis 3, we are reminded that nature was also cursed because of mankind's rebellion. And now nature, too, turned its back on this sorry scene. Man had corrupted nature through the Fall; now creation grieved as mankind advances the rebellion and kills the Creator.

Thus, nature hid its face. Darkness fell. Because at the cross, it looked like the darkness had won.

Satan, it seemed, had not only bruised the heel of the Anointed One, but had stolen a march and had crushed him completely. And the darkness symbolized this. Nature was mourning and grieving what humanity was doing.

Humanity was murdering God.

But it goes deeper still. Darkness also symbolizes judgement. Israel was under judgement. This is why the darkness covered the land of Israel. Where once it had been the Promised Land, now it had become the Cursed Land. The darkness was meant to serve as a sign of warning and judgement to the people of Israel just as it had been to the Egyptians enduring the final plague. God was passing judgement on the land *and the people* of Israel who, remember, had so recklessly accepted that curse at Jesus' trial in Pilate's Palace.

But it's deeper again than merely creation's grief and Israel's judgement.

The darkness expresses the fact that *God* was judging Jesus, his only begotten Son. The darkness is a visual reflection of what's happening on the cross. You see, on the cross, it was not just an innocent man dying for a political necessity. But rather, as Don Carson powerfully phrases it: "The Cosmic blackness hints at the deep judgement taking place."

Jesus, as we have seen, is God the Son made flesh. In chapter 1, we considered the wickedness of humanity. We saw that our nature desired that we would cruelly torture and torment the very Son of God. Sin reveled in the ripping of his flesh. Sin spat in his face with glee. Sin mocked his trauma with laughter.

But *all* of that paled in comparison to what God the Father was pouring on his beloved Son. In Isaiah 13:9, the prophet proclaimed that: "The day of the LORD is coming, *cruel*, with fury and burning anger, to make the earth a desolation and to destroy the sinners with it." Elsewhere he described Israel's punishment and said that they have "drunk from the hand of the LORD, the *cup of his wrath.*"

In Jeremiah 25:15, God spoke of the "wine cup of fury" that's in his hand. It's a frothing dark claret bubbling with his righteous rage and indignation. In Revelation, God speaks of the whore of Babylon, that great expression of human rebellion. And we read in Revelation 16:19 that that "great city was split into three parts, and the cities of the nations fell, and God remembered Babylon the Great, to make her *drain the cup of the wine of the fury of his wrath*," and promises that "anyone [who] worships the beast…will also drink the wine of God's wrath."

This wrath of God, the cup of frothing wine? That's the language of God's righteous hatred and anger and fury at man's rebellion. It symbolizes God's hatred towards sin. God *hates* sin with a furious rage because sin kills his children and destroys his creation. Sin has led this cosmic rebellion as the whip hand of Satan. Sin is personal revenge. And it's purposeful murder. Sin kills.

And God hates it.

This is why, dear friends, Christ suffered the hell of Hell on the hill of Calvary. You see, in the darkness, for *three whole* hours, Christ endured the punishment for sin that *we deserved*.

The fury of the wrath of God Most High.

Remember what our sin deserves: Death. But *then* imprisonment in Hell. For eternity, suffering the torment of the fires of judgement where there will be weeping wailing and gnashing of teeth. No mercy. No grace. No compassion. Just judgement. For eternity.

We deserve that. Because our sin is against the infinite holiness of God. In our rebellion, we have committed an infinite crime and justice demands we do the infinite time.

But in those three hours? The *infinite* God-man? Suffered our *infinite* Hell. Mine. He suffered what I *should* have suffered for *eternity*. And yours. He suffered what *you should* have suffered for *eternity*.

On the cross, his punishment was to experience *all* the judgement from God's righteous fury at our rebelliousness. In all its eternality. For three whole hours he endured what was a concentration of judgement the like of which could never begin to be understood or imagined.

The cross was where the righteous was made to suffer as the unrighteous.

Where the Holy was made to suffer as the unholy.

Where the innocent was made to suffer as the guilty.

Where the Person of the Son was made to suffer as the personification of Sin.

This is the horror of the cross. The true grotesque wickedness and violence of the punishment of the Son. And it lasted for three hours. Three hours which felt like infinite eternities.

Jesus was made accursed so that we could be made acceptable. When Jesus cried out that blood-curdling echo of Psalm 22, "*Eloi Eloi! Lama sabacthani*" (My God, My God! Why have your forsaken me?) we are meant to see this deeper judgement. In Zechariah 13 we read that there is a figure standing by the throne of the Father who is preparing to receive the sword of God. He is going to be stricken *by God*.

This is what was happening behind Jesus' cry. God, the Father, was forsaking the Son on the cross. Not because of a mission failed, but to win the victory that would redeem his people.

Now, this does not mean that the eternal Son was going to die. No; suffice it to say that Jesus died as still the same psychosomatically whole individual that he had been throughout his life. What *is* happening is that the divine Son isn't dead, but he is bearing the Father's wrath as God, as the Second Person of the Divine Trinity, so that the human guilt is placed upon him and borne by him in all its fullness. And so that, as a truly human man, he could indeed stand in our stead as our substitute.

He was given the guilt we deserve. He stood in our place as our substitute. And he bore the judgement and punishment that was meant for us.

What this means, dear friend, dear Christian, is that Jesus has *taken* your debt. That infinite cost which you have *earned* by being a sinner? On those bloodied shoulders, he took it upon himself. As Isaiah promised, "By *his stripes* we are healed" (Isaiah 53:5). We are healed spiritually and eternally. This means that Jesus *died as a substitute*. In our place.

He took the field of death instead of me. He took the punishment of God for sinfulness instead of me. He took the violence of man as murderers instead of me. And this means that the curse of sin? Of the Fall? That sting of death? *Finally*, at the cross and because of the cross, it was being unwound. It was being undone. And that means that we are free.

Christ became a prisoner so that slaves to sin could be freed.
Christ became a human so that humanity could be restored.
Christ became a convict so that guilty could be forgiven.
Christ became a corpse so that dead men could live.
Christ became *your* curse. For *your* sin. So that you could be redeemed.

When we live in our sin, and refuse to worship the king as he is, we are reveling in our sin. Even though we are rebels against God, and even as we are drinking the bitter gall of sin's poison, and even as we are letting sin bring us to spiritual and natural ruin, which is the consequence of sin being death, and even as we are *dying* from the sin that seeks to *devour* us? We *mock* the king who came to save us. We're quite literally these robbers on the crosses next to Jesus. We're terrorists against God's reign. And we deserve the death that Jesus died.

Look at Jesus. That is what *sin wants for you.* And it's what our sin deserves *from God.* And even as we're mocking Jesus, we're condemning ourselves as guilty for sinful treason against God. Just like Adam and Eve. Just like Satan.

But not like Jesus.

He's *the* king; not only of Israel, but of a greater Israel, a bigger kingdom, an eternal throne. But his Kingdom was forged in blood and sacrifice and death and crucifixion.

His trust in God was *so* strong that he labored *through* the suffering. God *didn't* deliver him *because* God had entrusted the path of deliverance to his faithfulness. Even to death on a cross.

Think of what this means for you in your life. Every sinful thought. Every bitter idea. Every resentful consideration. Every hurtful comment. Every gossiped slander. Every lustful glance. Every addicted high. Every selfish dollar spent. Every jealous action. Every single sin. Christ bore the curse for you. So that you could be freed from sin's horrendous slavery. By *his* death, *you* are healed. Healed from rebellion against God's rule. Healed from sinful hatred of God's reign. Healed from the implications of shame. Healed from the brokenness of sin's wounds.

You *are* healed. And you *will* reign with him in eternity.

By his death you have salvation, the forgiveness of sins.

By his death, you have righteousness despite being unrighteous.

By his death, you have redemption from Satan's realm.

By his death you have adoption into the family of God.

By his death you are freed from sin's power, shame's claims, Satan's lies, and the chains of evil.

By that bloodied, bruised, and beaten king, your curse is paid for.

Gaze upon Jesus with horror at what *our sin would do to Christ.* Yet gaze upon Jesus with joy at what *Christ has done to our sin.*

The cross of Christ is a very weird thing to venerate. We wear it on clothes, have jewelry depicting it, and even place it on the spires of our church buildings. And yet the cross is a horrific thing. It's a symbol of torture, of violence, and of victory of the strong over the week. In every cultural way, to the Romans, and the Jews, it was a sign, a symbol, of defeat.

But for the one who can truly see? It's the symbol of hope. Of life. Of triumph. Of redemption. Of strength. Of vitality. Of power. Of might. Of majesty. Of victory.

At the cross, the serpent was biting the heel of the king. But at the cross, the king was crushing the head of the serpent. And the curse was being undone.

But at what a cost. The *death* of the king.

The beatings. The nails. The thorns. The scourging. The suffocation. The weakness. The dehydration. This explains his sorrow and his suffering. It takes its toll. In Matthew 27:50 we read "Jesus cried out again with a loud voice and yielded up his spirit." He gave up his Spirit. With a *loud cry*. A shriek of anguish. And, at the moment of his choosing, beaten and violently tortured for hours, in the darkness, Jesus, the king, crucified by Gentiles, rejected by his people, and stricken by his Father, breathed his last, and died.

Jesus Has Conquered Your Sin

[Luke 23:44] *It was now the sixth hour and there was darkness over the whole land until the ninth hour,*

[45] *while the sun's light failed. And the curtain of the temple was torn in two.*

Accepted

The question that hangs over the entire crucifixion scene is this: Was it successful? You see, for the bystanders and onlookers? It looked like a *fait accompli*. The leaders had gotten what they wanted. The priests had killed Christ. Pilate had avoided a riot. The crowds had received their spectacle. Herod had gotten rid of a rival. All in all, for the government who'd been on his shoulders, oppressing him, it seems that they'd won. Jesus was very dead. Truly dead.

But *had* it *worked*? Had the curse been unwound? Had sin been defeated? Had the righteous wrath of God been propitiated, or satisfied, by Jesus' blood? In verses 44-45, we read that darkness was over the land of Israel for three hours. In those three hours, the infinite hell that we deserved was poured onto the infinite Son. The Father didn't turn his face away from his son; but he did turn his grace away. And the Son was isolated. Rejected. Judged. Condemned.

And then, as the frothing wine of God's judgement was drained down to the last dregs, the curtain of the temple tore. This often means little to us today. But for Israelites in the first century? That was a huge event. And it answers our question: Did Jesus' death work? *Yes!*

Where once God had chosen to hide himself from his people and restrict access to his presence, *now* access to him was once more granted. Where once only one man, on one day of the year, could go into one small chamber in the one holy Temple, the Holy of Holies? Now *anyone* can approach God and pray to him and *know* that God hears, and listens, and loves his people. Because of Jesus.

Because of Jesus, we get access to God. At the moment of the death of the King, there was a loud ripping noise in the temple. The vast, and heavy, veil that closed off the Holy of Holies from the rest of the world was torn. This was a *huge* event, even simply physically. The veil was about 60 feet high, possibly as thick as 4 inches, and was fashioned from blue, purple and scarlet material, twisted together with fine linen. Taking those details into consideration, the very fact that it was torn almost shows the supernatural power in and of itself.

But note that it was torn from the *top* down to the bottom. This is deeply poignant. And to understand it, we need to understand what Jesus' death achieved for us.

The Holy of Holies was where only one priest could enter, one time each year, to make atonement for sin. The curtain, or the veil, sealed God off from the world. But Jesus' death nullified that tradition. He *fulfilled* it. Now, his sacrifice had completed what every other sacrifice merely pointed to: His sacrifice, once for all, demonstrated the *end of the Temple age*, and the veil was torn to signify this. Never again would anyone have to find reconciliation with God through a burnt offering. They must come to the true Temple, Jesus, the king.

But even *more* than this, the fact that it's torn from the *top* reminds us that this is an act *of God*. It is God who therefore declares the Temple era finished.

Why?

Because God had *accepted* the sacrifice of Jesus in our place. Reconciliation, restoration of our relationship with God, returning to his presence has been made possible because of Jesus.

But even more than *this*, what we see by this is that access to God is no longer the prerogative of a priesthood set aside to work in a stone building. No. God has once more made himself accessible. Now access to God is through Jesus, for *any* and *all* who will believe. (This will be explored in greater depth in chapter 4.)

We don't come into the presence of God through music, through preaching, or through manufactured tears. We come to God and have access, unlimited, unadulterated, unbroken access, through Jesus. And Jesus alone. Because of Jesus we get to come before God. We get to come into the presence of God. And pray. And cry. And confess. And trust. And hope. And seek. And be forgiven. And be restored. And be comforted.

Christ won this for us. By his blood we are redeemed. Christian. You *are* forgiven. This is what you are. That is *who* you are. Positionally, you stand before God the Father as a son or a daughter of God. *Because of Christ.* There's no "maybe." No "what if." No "but." No caveat. This *is who you are.* Look around you when you're next in church. This is who we all are. A family adopted by God because of Christ. And because that's the case, and God had mercy on us? Then we can have mercy on one another. Because

God showed grace to us? We can show grace to each other. Because God forgave me? I can forgive you. Because God has loved you? You can love me. We can be kind. We can be gracious. We can be patient. We can be loving and forgiving.

So let's live like it. Let's live like we believe it. Let's live like we trust God who fulfilled Genesis 15 by tearing apart his own son on the cross to save you and me.

✞ Application: Beware the Wolves

But let us *also* be aware. The *main* opponents to Christ were not the Romans. In fact, the Roman centurion calls him a son of God. This is probably not a conversion, but it's certainly a mark of respect and an awareness of the uniqueness of Jesus' crucifixion. The point of the centurion's comment is to highlight something unique: The Gentile understood something that the Jews didn't.

The death of Jesus was larger, infinitely larger, than anything else he had ever seen. He had probably performed a hundred of these executions. Whether he was fully believing at this point or not, or even if he would do so later, is unknown. But the *contrast* is meant to be stark and poignant.

The Jews? Who *should have known* their Messiah? Mocked him even as they murdered him. But the Pagan Roman Gentile? He showed respect and was impressed by the manner and cosmic signs at Jesus' death.

So even more, this little detail, when combined with tearing of the veil, teaches us something about the New Covenant that Jesus inaugurated at his death. It tells us that the way into the Holy of Holies, or in other words, the way to God himself, has been opened, for *all* people, for all time, through Jesus the king.

At this moment, God was declaring that he would never again dwell in a temple made with hands, as we're told in Acts 17. And the gospel was conclusively confirmed as being for all people. This should not be a surprise to anyone who has read Genesis 3, or 12, or 15, or the Pentateuch, or the Prophets.

Because the *promise* has become a *reality*.

The cross delivered propitiation, the appeasing of the wrath of God. The cross brought redemption, the salvation from sin. The cross brought justification, the declaration of "innocent." The cross brought imputation, the transference of guilt to Jesus, and innocence to us. The cross brought reconciliation, the relationship once broken, now restored. The cross brought salvation, resurrection from spiritual death to spiritual life. The cross brought eternity, the New Creation a "now" reality. The cross fulfilled the Scriptures: Messiah has come, and his rule has begun. By the death of Christ, the death of Adam died. St. Athanasius said of the paradox of the crucifixion thus, that "the death of all was consummated in the Lord's body, yet, because the Word was in it, death and corruption were in the same act utterly abolished."

The cross achieved it all. And Christ achieved it *for all* who will believe.

This is our king.

This is Jesus. And this is what he died for. There's no *hint* or question that this could be a Plan B. No, this is the fulfilment of the Old Covenant. In his death, by his death, through his death, we, who are sinful, guilty rebels, have eternal *life*.

Do you grasp what he has achieved for us? Sin forgiven. Death defeated. Shame covered. The Strong Man bound. Evil vanquished. Jesus' Kingdom established. The Spirit promised.

All of this was won at Calvary, and it will be consummated upon his return. Evil is vanquished, but it has yet to be banished. But because of the cross, and the evidence of the resurrection, we know that it *will come to pass*. The Cosmic Rebellion has been dealt the death blow. It is defeated and awaiting destruction.

But who were the main enemies of the King? *Religious* leaders. Let us work hard to avoid ever being the reason why someone is blinded to Jesus. Let us never be needlessly offensive. Let us never be the cause for someone turning their face away from Jesus.

This means that we won't make Jesus fit inside our politics. He was bigger than Herod and Rome.

This means that we won't make Jesus fit inside our social constructions. He was bigger than the Laws of Moses.

This means that we won't make Jesus fit inside our national borders. He was bigger than Israel.

This means that we won't make Jesus look, sound, think, or reflect ourselves. He is bigger than you. He is bigger than me.

This means that we *will* preach Christ from Scripture. This means we *will* present Christ crucified and resurrected. This means we *will* provide the one, true, Gospel of faith alone, in Christ alone, received by grace alone, revealed in Scripture alone. And for that we will give glory to God alone.

✝ Application: You're A God-Killer

But if you've read this far and you're still reflecting on the sinfulness of your heart? And you've heard that your sin is a God-killer? And you resent the idea that Jesus died *to save you*? Then you need to hear one final thing from Luke:

> [Luke 23:39] *One of the criminals who were hanged railed at Him, saying, "Are you not the Christ? Save yourself and us!"*
>
> [40] *But the other rebuked him, saying, "Do you not fear God, since you are under the same sentence of condemnation?*
>
> [41] *And we indeed justly for we are receiving the due reward for our deeds; but this man has done nothing wrong."*
>
> [42] *And he said, "Jesus, remember me when you come into your kingdom."*
>
> [43] *And He said to him, "Truly I say to you, today you will be with me in Paradise."*

You have a choice to make. There have been many interpretations of Jesus. And there have been many reactions to Jesus. But all that matters, in this moment as you're reading these words, is that you have come face to face with Jesus himself through the Bible.

His own words, the Scriptures, tell you who he is. And you have a decision to make.

You.

Because everyone must respond to Jesus. Pilate lacked courage. The crowd lacked compassion. The priests lacked constraint. Herod lacked certainty. The soldiers lacked kindness. And Jesus? The only thing he lacked was a crime. He was *innocent*. And yet for our sake, he was made to be guilty. To die on the cross instead of us. To die as *your* substitute for *your* sin. To bring victory for you and to you.

Who will you listen to about Jesus? That he is God-made-flesh who died for *your* sins in *your* place. Society will deny it, but it cannot change it. Culture will attempt to redefine it, but they cannot affect it. Many around you will resent it, but they cannot avoid it. Jesus *did* die. He died in your place, as your substitute, so that *you* can be forgiven. So that you can be brought into the presence of God; indeed, so that you can enter into the *family* of God.

When I drive to college to teach every day, I pass a small sign which is extremely well meaning but I think not entirely helpful. It says: "Trust Jesus because hell is real." And that is true. But that is not the reason why we trust Jesus. We don't trust Jesus *to* avoid hell. We trust Jesus *and* avoid hell. But we trust Jesus *because* he took hell for us. Dear reader, don't trust Jesus because of fear; he conquered everything we have to be afraid of. We trust Jesus because he's the king. We trust Jesus because he loved us. Trust Jesus because he's *Jesus*.

Will you be like the first criminal on the cross? Looking for Jesus to be the wrong kind of king? Or will you see him for who He is? The sovereign Lord. The messiah. Whose death brings life?

What will be your reaction to Jesus?

Do you consider him innocent, but unimportant? Like Pilate?
Do you think he's a magician, but uninteresting? Like Herod?
Do you reckon he's a rebel, but undesirable? Like the crowd?
Maybe for you he's a revolutionary, but unsuccessful? Like Judas.
Perhaps you can call him a king, but unimpressive. Like the soldiers?

Or maybe you say, "Yes, *a* Messiah, but ultimately unable. Like the first criminal?

Or are you willing to say: "Yes, Jesus; you're innocent. *And* undefeated," like the second criminal. Will you know that, even though he died his kingdom *will* come. And he will reign forever as the king. Because although Jesus died, his death was acceptable and sufficient. To cover all your sins.

But at the end of our passage we are reminded that Jesus was dead. And his body was abandoned to the grave. Just like almost every single person who ever lived. That night, in fulfilment of Deuteronomy 21, a member of the Sanhedrin who was a follower of Jesus, Jospeh of Arimathea, went for the body, along with Nicodemus. They asked Pilate to give it to them and he gave his permission to retrieve the body. This tells us that Pilate didn't think Jesus committed high treason; for those who were executed for high treason would be left on the cross while their flesh rotted and was eaten by birds.

But Jesus was taken and wrapped in a linen shroud and placed in Joseph's own, as yet-unused, tomb. It was probably a mausoleum hewn from the cliff or rock face with an antechamber inside. There would have been shelves carved out of the walls where the bodies would rest. And there, in the cold, dark, earth, Jesus of Nazareth was buried. And as the rock was rolled over the entrance, darkness would have enveloped his corpse.

What chastising grief: the darkness of the tomb where the light of the world was buried. It was darker than even the earth had been when God had been pouring out his wrath on the Son. And outside, again, Matthew mentions the two Marys. They watched from a distance. Their world fallen apart just as their Lord had been torn apart.

Yet, under Roman law, they couldn't publicly grieve an executed criminal. They just watched in silent sadness. Witnesses to his murder. Watching his burial. And wondering: "What on earth happens now?"

Jesus was dead. Jesus was buried.

Was Messiah defeated?

If ever there was a moment in the cosmic rebellion, in Satan's coup, where it felt like, looked like, smelt like, God was thwarted. It was this moment.

God the Son, united to flesh, made to be sin for us, had been killed on a cross. He had been cursed by creation. Mocked by man. The suffering Servant. Satan watched, rejoicing at hearing that last, labored breath. After millennia, the serpent savored the moment of his victory.

Was Messiah defeated?

In answer to that question, Matthew's camera pans away.

The next morning, his view returns us to Pilate's chamber yet again where those conniving and cunning servants of the serpent were appealing to Pilate. Pilate must have been wondering, by this stage, would this issue of Jesus of Nazareth just never go away?

Oh how little he knew, right?

They say: "This guy claimed he'd rise from the dead after three days. If his stupid disciples steal his body? They'll claim his prophecy came true. And then it'll be even worse than before. Give us a guard. After three days, it'll *finally* go away."

Exasperated, Pilate says: "Take your own police and monitor it. I give you permission to secure it however you desire."

Thus, with yet more cruel snarls in place of smiles, the Chief Priests leave and seal the stone and set a guard at the tomb of Jesus of Nazareth. They had killed Jesus. They had buried Jesus. They had sealed Jesus up. They were guarding Jesus. Oh, they were sure, they had defeated Jesus!

Has the march of the king come to an end? He'd been broken. He'd been beaten. He'd been bruised. He'd been buried.

The cross was a battlefield! And Jesus had engaged the fight. As one commentator has phrased it: "The cross was his scaffold from one viewpoint, but his imperial chariot from another!"

Dead at the cross.

But the game's not over yet. In fact, *despite all appearances*, the greatest comeback in history is resting on the cusp. It looks like the king's defeated. But Satan had better not take his eye off the screen. Third quarter's over; but there's a long fourth quarter to play.

And although Friday ended in death.

Sunday's coming.

Chapter 3:

...Because of the Resurrection[5]

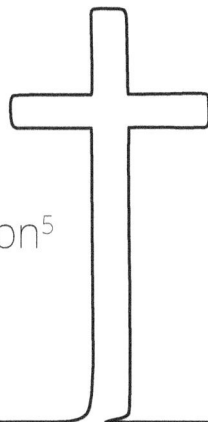

[Luke 24:5] *"Why do you seek the living among the dead?*

[6] *He is not here, but has risen. Remember how he told you, while he was still in Galilee,*

[7] *that the Son of Man must be delivered into the hands of sinful men and be crucified and on the third day rise."*

Introduction

Have you ever experienced a victory? A real victory? A true victory? Maybe you remember the last time USC dominated Clemson? Maybe you remember the last time Clemson destroyed USC? Or whatever your sports equivalent is: The Old Firm, a London derby, *el classico*, Federer versus Nadal, Duke versus North Carolina, the Yankees versus the Red Sox, and so on. Perhaps you remember *your* own, personal, victory. A triumph in your spelling bee? Winning a promotion at work?

Those victories feel great. They bring bragging rights and highlight reels that you could watch and rewatch and the dopamine rush always hits. But as every coach will tell you: The work begins

---

5   This sermon was crafted using a chapter from my book *"Take and Eat": From Fall to Feast*, also published by Energion. There will be some overlap here, but that book is a larger, broader delve into the Biblical storyline from Genesis to Revelation.

again tomorrow. Those victories? They feel good. They taste great. But they pass away pretty quickly, don't they?

Maybe you can remember the last truly great victory in civilization, when the Berlin Wall fell in 1989? The Triumph of the West against Communism. When it felt like we were entering into a wonderful new era of world peace, prosperity, and harmony: Every hippy's dream! And yet...what happened? It never *really* came. And that utopia? It didn't last. The work had to continue. Life? It continued just as it had the day before.

Such triumphs, such victories? They're *good*. They're *nice*. But in reality...*nothing truly changes*. Life goes on *as it had before*. Those victories grow distant. They reside in a past that is ultimately beyond us. And nothing has ultimately changed.

That being said, there's something truly *special* about a *comeback* victory. That's a whole different level of enthusiasm and excitement.

Perhaps the most noticeable such victory I remember was the first Superbowl I watched in this country. Do you remember the Superbowl from 2017? That was quite a game. Tom Brady's Patriots faced off against the Falcons. At the end of the first quarter? Atlanta 7. Brady 0. At the end of the second quarter? Atlanta 21. Brady 0. At the end of the third quarter? Atlanta 28. Brady 9.

I remember sitting in my friend's chair thinking: "I mean, all this Brady talk? Seems a bit overblown." In fact, I was giving quite a bit of sassy chat to my Patriots friends, which was quite irrational because I was someone who literally knew nothing about American Football.

But from my vantage point? The patriots looked weak. Their defense was more vulnerable than a British Ship in Boston Harbor. They were leaky. Sloppy. Frankly, they looked doomed. What was the point of even finishing the fourth quarter as a Patriots fan? I mean, really? It's game over. Call it already. It's clearly done and dusted. Like some Patriots fans, leave the game early and be home in time for tea.

If we stop reading the gospel accounts too early, it's like we're those Patriot fans. If we put the book down at Luke 23:46, we're going to think that the game was over. The jig was up. Defeat was imminent. In fact, further than that, it would be quite clear that defeat *had* come. The whistle's blown. And the king? Well, there's no coming back from this.

Why? Because as Satan watched and as the Chief Priests mocked, Jesus bowed his head.

And died.

And it definitely looked like the king was defeated. But just like me in 2017, Satan had better not take his eyes off the screen. Because it wasn't over yet.

In this chapter, we're going to consider and reflect on the resurrection of Christ. But to do that, we must first return to the *grave* of Christ. Mark records, in chapter 15 the following:

[43] *Joseph of Arimathea, a respected member of the Council, who was also himself looking for the Kingdom of God, took courage and went to Pilate and asked for the body of Jesus.*
[44] *Pilate was surprised to hear that he should have already died. And summoning the centurion, he asked him whether he was already dead.*
[45] *And when he learned from the centurion that He was dead, he granted the corpse to Joseph.*

The King Was Dead

We return to the *tomb* because, importantly, the king *was* dead. Christ had been unjustly executed. Reviled by criminals. Rejected by his own people. Forsaken by his Father. And now he was dead. Mark's point was that Jesus died as the suffering servant, alone, rejected, and yet for the sins of the world. He had indeed fulfilled his mission.

But he was still dead.

And Joseph of Arimathea wanted to bury Jesus. But because Jesus was technically a political prisoner, executed for treason, the body was meant to remain in Roman custody. This is why, as we saw in the last chapter, Joseph had to go to Pontius Pilate and get Roman authority to reclaim the body. And Pilate, no doubt, stared at Joseph for a moment…confused.

"Wait, really? That was but a few hours ago! He died already?"

Indeed, so seemingly surprised was Pilate, that he summoned the Centurion to ascertain the truth. Was Joseph lying and actually trying to *preserve* Jesus? Had the Centurion *botched* the execution? Thus, the Centurion was beckoned, and he explained that Jesus was indeed dead. He had died swiftly, and it had been confirmed with a spear through the heart.

Jesus. Was. Dead.

Which is the point that Mark is at pains to emphasize, isn't it? The king really was dead. Joseph saw it. Pilate doubted it. But the centurion confirmed it. And the corpse proved it.

Jesus was dead. He wasn't *sort of dead*. He wasn't *mostly* dead like the comical scene from *The Princess Bride*. No, Jesus was *dead* dead. This is a very important point because it points us back to Genesis 15. There, God made a covenant with Abram. God had already made promises to Abram about land and descendants, but time had passed. Thus, in chapter 15 Abram asked God: "How shall I know that I am to possess the land?" In response, God told Abram to bring certain animals before him:

[Gen. 15:10] *And he brought him all these, cut them in half, and laid each half over against the other. But he did not cut the birds in half.*

So a channel or a pathway was created. It was a bloody, gruesome sight. It was also relatively common in the ancient world. Abram knew what was taking place. This was to be a blood covenant of fealty and loyalty. The promise was this: They would walk through the pathway together and if either party *breaks* the covenant, that individual would become like the animals – broken in a bloody mess. Torn apart.

God was making a promise to Abram. *God* would pay the ultimate punishment if the *promise* did not come to pass. But Abram understood that *his* descendants would be cut apart if they disobeyed the *terms and conditions* of the covenant. But then something strange happened. In verse 17 we read this:

[17] *When the sun had gone down and it was dark, behold, a smoking firepot and a flaming torch passed between these pieces.*

Do you see the significance? What happened? God *took upon himself all* the responsibilities of the covenant punishment. This is why the cross is so important. Jesus, the God-man, was killed to fulfil Genesis 15. The covenant *broken by the sons of God*, Israel, has been paid for by the *only begotten Son of God*. Now, in Christ, those promises of restoration, of peace, of reconciliation with God can be fully experienced for *all* who will believe. Jesus was torn apart to honor God's promise to Abram.

But the point remains: Jesus *was* dead. In fact, just as *God* had planned.

Corpse Released and Buried

And so, as an act of benevolence, Pilate granted the request. The body was handed over to Jospeh of Arimathea. He took it and wrapped it in a linen cloth and prepared to place it in his tomb. As Joseph led a fourth and final procession of Jesus through the city and out to the grave, the two Marys watched. To prepare, at sunset of the Sabbath, they went and bought spices, and then, first thing the next morning they would go and wash the body and say their final goodbye.

We know and have already seen that the Chief Priests had convinced Pilate to seal the tomb and give his permission for them to set a watch on the tomb. The Chief Priests certainly didn't think that Jesus would rise from the dead. Of course not. But they *did* think that it was possible that the followers may *believe* that had happened *should the body go missing*. Or perhaps even that they might perpetuate the fraud by *stealing* the body themselves.

Thus, the Chief Priests had told Pilate that if there were to be a serious breach of the moral code and the disciples did commit the ultimate taboo of robbing the grave? Well, those morons, those common plebs, those uneducated religious idiots? They'd *believe* that the criminal had actually risen from the dead!

"We know, Pilate, such things don't happen. But they're incredulous fools! So best let us *be sure* nothing malign happens," they say, their tongues dripping with malevolent sarcasm. And thus Pilate, no doubt exasperated and annoyed at this never ending Jesus scandal, gave them permission and, no doubt impolitely, told them to get lost.

And this is what our society and culture, generally, thinks of us Christians, right? That we're incredulous, gullible, fools. That we're either morons or bigots for taking Jesus at his word. And yes, it's absolutely true that we fail so often to observe and live up to his ideals and his standards. But we believe what he's said. About himself. And his mission.

But society? It likes to domesticate Jesus. It'll gladly speak of Jesus as "a great man", a good chap, just like Thomas Jefferson presented in his chopped-up Bible. Jefferson had been heavily influenced by the Enlightenment. This was a movement that rejected *revelation* for *reason* (so called at any rate). Because of his scientific *reason*, Jefferson took his scissors to the Bible and began to cut away all the things in it that he thought were fake. He didn't hate the Bible. He certainly often spoke highly of it. He even said that the teachings of Jesus were "the most sublime and benevolent code of morals which has ever been offered to man."

And yet.

When he died, the chopped-up Jefferson Bible was published. And it was revealed that he had redacted and omitted the supernatural conception of Jesus, all of Jesus' miracles, any hint of reference to Jesus' divinity, and the resurrection. Thomas Jefferson is a modern *epitome* of the Chief Priests we're going to consider below. They looked into the very face of their Messiah. And they responded: "No." Because they, like Jefferson, rejected Jesus as *he presented himself.* Jefferson's Jesus may have been a very nice chap who showed compassion for the sick, but he was not the king.

Likewise, our society will gladly extol the virtues of the well-meaning "Communist Jesus" aka the "Robin Hood Jesus": Take from the rich, give to the poor. He had some really nice ideas. He was a really sweet dude: "Couldn't work, of course. But good intentions, all the same," they patronizingly sneer.

Society will even delightedly take Jesus' words out of context, just like the Devil. "Love is love. God is love. Therefore, love however you want." That's fine, right? Jesus wants you to be happy. Just make Jesus into your own image. He'll like what you like, permit what you want, and ignore your flaws and failures. And rebellion.

But Jesus *is not a domesticated* king. He is *the* king.

And Christian there are liars out there and there are wolves in sheep's' clothing within the church who *pretend* to be ambassadors for Jesus. False prophets and deceivers who stand on pulpits and who post on social media that you can literally *buy* favors from God. One such scam doing the rounds around the time of this writing was that for a mere one thousand bucks you could get your *own special guardian angel.* That's the prosperity gospel. And it's a *lie.* Jesus suffered the cross *before* the vindication. The cross. The wickedness of man. The wrath of God. He *endured* it. To think that we can buy our way out of following our Lord is an *insult* to his suffering.

Jesus is *not* domesticated. Jesus is the King. Let us never forget that. As C.S. Lewis memorably stated in the *Chronicles of Narnia* about Aslan, the Christ-figure: "He's not safe. But he is good."

With Pilate's permission granted, therefore, the Chief Priests slapped themselves on the back. Mission accomplished. Jesus, the imposter, the pretender, the traitor.

Was dead.
Was buried.
His tomb was guarded.
His tomb was sealed.

And in a few days this would all be finally over. The rabble would go home and it would all be forgotten.

Because Jesus, they knew, they were certain, they had ensured, was dead.

And time passed. The friends and family of Jesus huddled together over Sabbath. They shared their griefs. And they shared their fears. "He's gone," they whispered, still confused and shocked. Would there be reprisals from the priests? From Pilate? They tried not to think about it.

But it was a long Sabbath. Finally, they fell into a restless sleep.

Early the next morning, Mark tells us, when the sun had risen, the two Marys made their way to the tomb, sadness in their hearts. All the finagling and shenanigans between Pilate and the Chief Priests had happened without their knowledge. They were on their way to the tomb simply because they were desperate to give the broken, dead body of their friend, their Messiah, the dignity of proper funeral rites. But as they got closer, they realized that the very large stone had been moved aside.

What had happened? Matthew's gospel fills in some details that Mark omitted. We learn from Matthew 27 that there had been an earthquake. And the mighty stone that had been rolled to cover the doorway? Had moved. The seal had broken, and the stone had rolled away from the tomb's entrance.

Whether the angel used the earthquake, or the earthquake was because of his arrival, we aren't sure. But the angel of God descended from heaven and the stone was rolled away. Now, you might be thinking, this is a mythical way of explaining a natural phenomenon. And, at face value, I'd be willing to give you that.

If Matthew stopped there.

But he doesn't. What happens next? The angel sat and waited. And watched. I imagine him, and this is just me (it's not in the text), but I picture him on top of the stone, legs waggling as he waited with excited eagerness.

Remember, this isn't any regular guy; we actually get a description. Matthew heard from the women what the angel looked like. He was like lightening. Radiant. Pure. Electrifying. Shimmering. Holy. His clothing was white as snow.

So, what's going on here in this scene? Matthew's giving us the eyewitness account. The earthquake wasn't a natural phenomenon; this was a spiritual event. It was a divine action. And the angel remained to speak with the women.

But what about the guards? They had been such a crucial part of that oh-so-cleverly-devised plan by the Chief Priests. Well, they weren't much use: They'd *fainted* in fear. They were so terrified at the arrival of this majestic, lightening-like figure, and his ability to move the stone, that they staggered in terror. The angel's confidence in the face of their little daggers and swords terrified them such that they simply collapsed. And that means they didn't hear what happened next.

But before we move on, I want to make one further point about the earthquake. In Exodus 19, we read from Moses that God was making a covenant, a vow, with Israel. In that covenant, the terms were that if they obeyed the covenant God would bless them. They would be God's treasured people and a light to the world for true worship. In Exodus 19:9 we read the following:

[9] *And the Lord said to Moses, "Behold, I am coming to you in a thick cloud, that the people may hear when I speak with you, and may also believe you for ever."*

After the people dedicated themselves, consecrated themselves, and made themselves as pure as possible we then read the following:

[16] *On the morning of the third day there were thunders and lightnings and a thick cloud on the mountain and a very loud trumpet blast, so that all the people in the camp trembled.*
[17] *Then Moses brought the people out of the camp to meet God, and they took their stand at the foot of the mountain...*

Much later in redemptive history, the storyline of the Bible, we read in 1 Kings chapter 19 the following:

> [11] *And he said, "Go out and stand on the mount before the Lord."* *And behold, the Lord passed by, and a great and strong wind tore the mountains and broke in pieces the rocks before the Lord, but the Lord was not in the wind. And after the wind an earthquake, but the Lord was not in the earthquake.*
>
> [12] *And after the earthquake a fire, but the Lord was not in the fire. And after the fire the sound of a low whisper.*
>
> [13] *And when Elijah heard it, he wrapped his face in his cloak and went out and stood at the entrance of the cave. And behold, there came a voice to him and said, "What are you doing here, Elijah?"*

What do these passages tell us? There are more like them, especially in the prophets. We learn that earthquakes and dramatic environmental phenomena, in certain circumstances, accompany the *arrival* of *God*. And this shapes what's happening at the tomb.

Mary and Mary? They felt the earthquake. We don't know at what time exactly they arrived to see what happened. But we know they felt the quake because they reported it later to Matthew. And their theological Spidey senses were tingling.

Because *something* was happening.

They didn't know what it was, yet. But they were going to find out. And they encountered the man of electrifying appearance seated on the stone. He told them not to fear.

Not to fear? Soldiers are passed out on the ground in front of them. The tomb's wide open. And *you're* terrifying, Mr. Stranger!

What on *earth* was going on?

Entering the Tomb

I love trying to imagine this scene. Perhaps they looked around, unsure about what was happening. They didn't seem to *see* anyone else, and yet the grave where they had *seen* Joseph inter Jesus' body was indeed open. Slowly, carefully, with trepidation in their hearts, they walked towards it.

Maybe one of them peered in, and then, breath bated, stepped in. The other followed. And they stopped.

Confused.

They looked at the table, or the shelf where the body ought to have been, and there they see another young man dressed in a white robe.

They're startled at his presence. They're alarmed. They watched as he slowly raised his head and looked directly at them. His eyes seemed to pierce their very soul.

They held their breath.

A pregnant pause.

An interminable silence.

Aeon of aeons felt like it passed.

The moment felt like an eternity.

Suddenly, he opened his mouth to speak.

And everything.

EVERYTHING.

Changed.

Comeback King: The Resurrection Changes Everything

[6] *And he said to them, 'Do not be alarmed. You seek Jesus of Nazareth, who was crucified. He has risen; He is not here. See the place where they laid Him.*

[7] *But go, tell His disciples and Peter that He is going before you to Galilee. There you will see Him, just as He told you.'*

[8] *And they went out and fled from the tomb, for trembling and astonishment had seized them, and they said nothing to anyone, for they were afraid.*

The Stranger Reveals His Purpose

They tried to listen and comprehend his words but their minds would have been going a million miles an hour. Nevertheless, they heard him clearly, his deep, rich voice echoed gently through the tomb. His first words were to comfort them, although, as we read, to little effect.

"Do not be alarmed," he said. Which was certainly a very nice sentiment.

But place yourself into the sandals of these women. The body of Jesus, a political prisoner executed for treason, appeared to be missing. And this man was in the tomb and almost accused them that they were seeking this Jesus. That would feel intimidating, right?

But he continued speaking. And here we have the first, and only, full declaration of the complete gospel message in Mark's account. And perhaps what is so shocking and remarkable about Mark's account is that it is so nonchalant.

This figure says: "He is risen! He is not here." Such simple, short sentences, and yet they contain the truth that all of the cosmos has changed.

✝ Application: The Resurrection Paradigm

Jesus, by His resurrection, has brought a New Creation paradigm to rule on this world. The kingdom of God has come, because the king has defeated death and is alive, though being killed! And this changes *everything*.

Throughout the Old Testament there were numerous moments of "re-creation." After the expulsion from Eden. After the Fall. After the flood. After the Exodus. After the exile. Each of those moments had been bursting with potential. New life, new hope, new expectations. And each time the hope had faded because sin persisted. Sin's cruel tyranny had invaded the post-Eden world. Sin had snuck onto the ark. Sin had spread like yeast throughout God's Israel. No matter where you look in the Old Testament, no matter which hero you look at, their life always ends in that universal disappointment: Death. Because no matter how righteous they may have been, they were sinners. And death is the consequence of sin.

But now, this king, Jesus, has brought about the true and final New Creation. So long as Christ is alive and reigns on the throne, his people, his church, will never truly die. And, because of the resurrection, we know that he has defeated death itself. This means that his kingdom will be eternal. Yes, it awaits the culmination and consummation upon his return, but it *has been* inaugurated and active by his resurrection. He *is* risen. And this changes everything.

And Christian, this matters to you and me. It means that we can be confident in our future because we can be certain about our salvation. The promises of eternal life have been sealed by his blood and delivered through His resurrection. By faith we are united to the resurrected Christ. This is the doctrine of union with Christ. And because of this, we are *in* Christ, and all the spiritual blessings that God has promised are ours through Jesus. Not because of us, or anything in us, but because of Jesus.

Thus, we have access to the resurrection power of Christ through the same Spirit who now indwells us. And the Spirit of Christ brings with him the power to change us. He can change how we think. He can change how we act. He can change how we worship. He can change our relationships. He changes how we grieve, how we cry, how we suffer. He changes how we prioritize time, money, and the years of our life.

The resurrection, brought to bear on us by the work of the Holy Spirit, changes everything.

Christian, the question that Mark challenges us with is this: Are you living in light of the resurrection? This world is fleeting. Like our youth, it *will* come to an end. But eternity? That is guaranteed. And it is long. But we're already tasting eternity because the power of sin over us has destroyed. We're no longer enslaved to sin, but to Christ.

So Mark asks us: Are we living in light of the resurrection? Does the reality, the cosmic, eternal, majestic, and assuring reality of the resurrection impact you personally? Do you want to live a life of discipleship? Of *resurrectional* discipleship? Do you want to live a life of obedience? Enabled by the *resurrection* power of Christ? Do you want to live a life of worship? Inspired and purposeful because of the *resurrection* power of Christ?

Or are you really, truly, honestly content to simply turn up and play the game? Once or twice a year at Christmas or Easter, if you're honest? To pay false lip service? To put in half-hearted effort?

And what about you, dear unbelieving friend? You've made it halfway through the book. Superb. I hope you're enjoying it and finding it illuminating. But in this moment, with the gentlest will in the world, I want you to think about the gospel.

Christ died for you. But if you're not a believer in the life, death, and resurrection of Christ? If you're not serving him as king? If you're not living for him as your Lord? Then showing up occasionally? Giving to the offering in church when you do turn up? Standing to sing the (sometimes terrible) songs?

None of that will save you, dear friend.

Only Jesus can save you. And *only* Jesus *will* save you.

Your best efforts? Won't save you.

Your best hopes? Won't save you.

Your money, your curiosity, your occasional "doffing of the cap"? Won't save you.

Christ demands all from you because Christ gave all for you.

Dear friend, your sin is more than just as bad thing. It's a chasm, a wall, a gulch too wide and deep for you to ever cross. Sin is anti-God. It's *sin* that placed Christ on the cross. Sin, we saw, was saying to the God who offered you life, love, forgiveness, restoration, and adoption: "No!" Our sin is our heart saying: "I want you to die because I want to be God."

Yet, friend, Jesus says *back to you*: "I *did* die."

"And you're *still not God*."

"I Am."

"And I'm willing to show you my grace. To forgive you. If you will repent from your sinful rebellion against me and instead turn to me, I will save you. You can rest inside my sacrifice. You can be restored to my heavenly Father. Turn from your God-killing sin and instead become a God-adopted son. Let God transform you from a slave of Sin to a saved son: A child of God himself.

Friend, Christ died your death so that you don't have to experience the justice your sin deserves. But you have to accept that offer. You have to live in that grace. *Knowing* about the offer? That doesn't save you. If you're drowning? You *know* a life jacket can save you. But it'll do nothing for you if you don't use it. If you're in a crash? You *know* a parachute can save you. But not if you won't use it. If you're going to be judged and go to Hell? You *know* Christ can save you. But not if you won't follow him.

Will you do so right now as you're reading this? Will you follow him and accept his death in your place? Receive his grace? Or do you want to take your chances on your own?

And Christian, let me take this moment to ask each of us why we do the 'rituals' of the Christian tradition? Do you attend church because you're 'expected' to be there? Christmas and Easter, you go to church because that's 'just what you do?' Maybe you're a regular attender because the music gives you an emotional high? Maybe you go because you like your preacher? Or the praise team? Or maybe you go to church just because you know you *should* be there. Sort of like emotionally blackmailing yourself to *feel* spiritual?

If so, dear friend, that's like you're coming to worship a dead god. That was the attitude of the Marys. Yes, they were *passionate*, and, yes, they were *loyal*, and, yes, they were going to give Jesus appropriate homage and *respect*. But they were going to anoint a *corpse*.

But when believers gather, we don't gather to *remember* a dead king. We come to *worship* the resurrected king. We come to *worship* through the singing of Christ-exalting songs, through prayers of repentance, praise, and intercession, through the public reading of Scripture, through the proclamation of his Word *because* he is alive.

The women prepared to go to the tomb to anoint their dead Jesus. But they left with a completely different mission. Theirs were the first lips to taste the sweetness of the message of the resurrection. And their mission? It's ultimately why *you're* at church: To be *equipped* to go out from the building, the gathering, with the hope and message of the gospel, to bring it to a lost and dying world. The gospel is not a nice story of a heartwarming sacrificial example, but one of cosmic, eternal, and absolute victory. We are commissioned to be evangelists, ambassadors, spokespersons for the *king*. To be laborers for the Kingdom. To be in business to support the Kingdom. To be nurses who are the hands and feet of the Kingdom. To be thinkers, debaters, preachers, teachers, story tellers, musicians, and videographers for the Kingdom. Wherever the Lord has placed you, you are *there* to be Christ's witnesses in that place.

Every Sunday you leave the Christian gathering at church having been discipled and built up in Christ. But *more* than that, you go out from there *commissioned by one another* and by the Spirit of Christ, having been discipled to *grow in Jesus* and to *go with Jesus*.

While the women were terrified in the tomb, the angel bade them go and see where the body had once rested. There they indeed saw that the plinth was definitely empty. The linen shroud had been neatly folded where his head had lain. And they didn't quite realize it yet, but the tomb hadn't been opened to *let Jesus out*. It had been opened to *let them in*. To see the evidence for themselves.

Christian, as we eavesdrop on their conversation, we, too, are bade to come and see. Come to Scripture and see what God says about his king, about Jesus. Come and see. Look at the empty tomb. Jesus *is not there*. The tomb *is empty*. He has risen.

Come and see, beloved brother and sister. Your king, whom you follow and serve, and strive to be like? He is risen. He is alive. Come and see. Explore the tomb. Explore scripture. Explore and see for yourself.

And then? And then *go and tell*, Christian. Be *bold*. This is *the hope* and truth the foundation of our faith. Shout it from the rooftops! Don't be embarrassed. Don't be afraid to share the hope of the resurrection of Jesus with the world.

Because Jesus is alive. Don't be embarrassed by it. We *know* that people don't typically rise from the dead. We aren't gullible fools. We know how death works. But *that's the point*. *People* don't rise from the dead. Therefore, the empty tomb is explained by the fact that Jesus? Isn't any ordinary person. He's the king. And although he was dead, the tomb is empty because he is risen from the dead.

And Matthew tells us that we have witnesses: These women, and soon there'll be Peter and John and then others; indeed, even the temple police (when they wake up). They'll *all* acknowledge the tomb is empty.

So don't be embarrassed; proclaim it boldly. This is the deeper truth, the deeper reality. Come and see. Look for yourself. Remind yourself of the gospel. Of the resurrection. And then preach it to yourself and proclaim it to the world.

The tomb is empty.

Mark asks you. Are you truly ready? Are you truly living in light of the resurrection?

Are you truly captivated by the cross?

Are you truly energized by the resurrection?

Are you truly heeding the ministry and guidance of the Holy Spirit?

Are you a disciple of Jesus desperate to be obedience to his Great Commission? So that "as you are going, you're baptizing converts in the name of the Father, Son and Holy Spirit, *teaching them to obey all that Christ has commanded you*?" How can you be teaching others to obey all his commands if you aren't transfixed in humble awe at the glory of the resurrection? By what power can you call them to obedience? To worship? To repentance? These women were given a command to go and to tell others that Jesus is risen.

We've been given the same command. Are we going to be obedient?

A Familiar Stranger

Yet, we read that they were afraid. And because they were afraid, they told no one about what they had heard. At least, initially. Which perhaps takes us by surprise, considering the magnitude of the stranger's words. But the contrast in Mark is between humanity as a whole and Jesus.

In the last few chapters of Mark, we witnessed politicians play with Jesus' life as if it were nothing more than a poker chip in a game of thrones. We witnessed religious leaders sell their souls to the world and deny their true king and Messiah. We watched the closest of his disciples reject, forsake and desert him. We observed nature itself darken in mourning at the death of its Creator. And *now* we watch as these women flee in fear at the words of the angel in the tomb.

Humanity. In all its pomp, in all its frailty, in all its arrogance, in all its misplaced loyalty. Failing. What about you? How have we responded to the gospel? Are there idols that captivate you and keep you from worshipping the Lord as you should? What is it that you love more than Christ? Your relationship? Your money? Your comfort? Your entertainment? Your job? Your sense of purpose? Your worldview? Your theological system? Your ideas? Your preferences? A mis-ordered worship is *sinful*. It's worshipping at the altar of death. Take them all and crucify them, so that your worship can be for Christ alone.

Look at our king on the cross. His soul was tossed into deep, heart-wrenching sorrow, a loneliness and isolation we can't even begin to imagine. And he went through this, because of *our* sin: All of our anger. All our bitterness. All our hatred. All our rebellion. All our jealousy. All our lust. All our slander. All our gossip. All our envy. All our greed. All our bullying. All our oppression. All our violence. All our drunkenness. All our addictions. All of it. He knows the suffering of it. And he calls us to hate it as he hates it.

Christian, do we take the Hell of Calvary too lightly? Do the actions of our lives reflect a genuine horror at what our sin did to Christ? Or do the actions of our lives betray a heart that, in reality, doesn't really care? Christ suffered hell so that we might savor heaven. But, oh, Christian, at *what* a cost. Jesus' own body broken. Jesus' perfect blood spilt on that cursed tree.

The ladies obey the command to leave and go to the other disciples. No doubt their emotions were running into hyperdrive. The horror of the murder of Jesus on the cross. The grief all through Sabbath. The angel's words echoing through their heads. We can only imagine what on earth they were thinking. As they departed from the tomb, with joy and fear in their hearts, they ran to tell the disciples.

And then they slid to a stop.

Because standing in the track in front of them was a familiar face.

Familiar, yet something different. It took a second, perhaps, to register. After all, the last time they'd seen this face, it was little more than a bloody pulp. But he greeted them.

And everything changed again. Everything they barely dared to hope and believe was confirmed.

The tomb was empty, yes; but it was empty *because Jesus is alive.* This was no mirage, no grief-caused ghost, no sleep-deprived-addled mistake. They fell at his feet. And they *touched* him. You can't touch an hallucination.

And they worshipped him.

Why?

The earthquake had prepared them to realize that something was happening. Now they understood: *God was coming.* And so they worshipped God. Risen from the dead.

And as they worshipped, with tears flowing rapturously down their faces, their minds scrambled to make it all make sense. To put the pieces together.

But everything changes because Jesus is alive. The old rules are upended. The old norms have changed. Everything that God had promised throughout the entire Old Testament had brought time and nature to this singularity. All of Scripture had pointed to this moment.

Adam in the Garden of Eden pointed forward to Jesus in gardens outside Jerusalem. The promised serpent crusher of Genesis 3:15 had come and the wages of our sin, which is death, has been conquered by this greater Adam.

Noah and his ark pointed forward to Jesus being the ark of the New Covenant. All who take refuge in the resurrected Lord and the work of his cross and resurrection will avoid the wrath of God for our sinfulness.

Abraham pointed forward to the tearing apart of God for breaking the covenant. And Jesus had been *brutally* torn apart. But he is the true promised offspring who would bless *all* the nations of the world.

Israel pointed forward to an obedient Son; but every son of Adam was sinful. But Jesus? He obeyed even to the point of death, as a slave, as the very personification of sin. He was the one True Israelite.

David pointed forward to a king who would reign eternally from an eternal throne over a never-ending Kingdom which would never be shaken. Jesus, the resurrected king, is that king. His reign will never end. His Kingdom will never cease. His throne stands above all time.

Isaiah spoke of a stump of Jesse and an offspring, a seed, who would grow and blossom from the old, chopped down, tree of Israel. This offspring, this shoot of Jesse, is Jesus. A greater David. A triumphant David. A sinless David. An *eternal* David.

Because the tomb had been opened. And Christ is triumphant. He's the fulfilment of it all. The resurrection is the vindication of Jesus's work. It tells us that God had accepted the sacrifice and that we can therefore be forgiven.

Talk about a comeback.

Christian, consider what this means. This is the source, the foundation of our hope. Because *Jesus* was raised, *we* will be raised. Because *Jesus* was raised in a new and perfect body, *we* will be raised into a new and perfect body. Because *Jesus* was raised to reign, *we* will be raised to reign. Because *Jesus* was raised to eternal life, *we* will be raised to eternal life.

Death is *not* the end. It may swallow our temporal bodies; but it will never swallow our new creation bodies. This means that the very sting of death, that terrifying sense of inevitability and futility? Is gone. Death is dead because Jesus is alive.

And we now see that the *tomb* of the Old Creation?

Was nothing more than the *womb* of the New Creation.

Jesus is the firstborn of the New Creation, the New Covenant life. And this is *all* ours, given to us as a gift, if we but bow down and worship the Lord of Life. The implications of this resurrection life are immense.

When you pray? You don't pray to an inanimate block of wood or stone or gold, like the idols of old. Nor do you pray to a dead and rotting corpse of useless men like the saints, or like the Buddha. Nor do you pray to a myth like Vishnu. No. You pray to a risen king. A *listening* lord. Who is able to help you. Who was seen and touched as evidence of his resurrection. Why would you pray to *any other being or person*? What can they do? They can't hear you; they're dead. But we pray to the *risen Lord*. He hears. He listens. He loves. And he helps. And he knows.

When you cry? You cry to a king who has cried tears of anguish and grief and sadness and pain. He empathizes with you. And because he *knows*, he can help you.

When you struggle? He's powerful enough to conquer death. He can help you in your moments of weakness and pain and isolation.

When you fail? He encourages you with the voice of a brother, and the strength of a king, and the tenderness of a friend.

When you're afraid? He experienced fear deeper than we can imagine; he sweat drops of blood. He can comfort you.

When you're lost? He can guide you.
When you're rejoicing? He celebrates with you.
When you sing? He basks in joy.
When you dance? He smiles with delight.
When you obey? He laughs with glee!

How can this be? Only *because he lives.* He's not a corpse in the tomb. He's not given over to corruption. He's not broken and bruised anymore. He's risen. He's able. He's powerful. He has conquered. He is alive. So come to him. He hears you. Cling to him. He helps you. Trust him. He's proven himself. This is your king!

Christ was in Control

Let us take a moment here, to remind ourselves that Jesus knew what he was doing. He stood before kings and priests and governors with quiet confidence. He touched the sick and dying. He healed the leprous and the lame. He loved the unlovable. He sat with the unclean. He forgave the sins of those who repented. He went to the cross and suffered the ignominy and the shame and the humiliation therein. He experienced the rejection of his own people. He faced the castigation of the Gentiles who crucified him. He knew the torment of the demons as they mocked him. And finally, he understood the eternal wrath of the Father as God's sword of justice was thrust into him.

And he died.

And his friends and family? They grieved. Grief is a deep cavern that no one else can fully comprehend or begin to grasp. Your experience will be unique to you. Grief is the loneliest place in the world. We do not deal with grief like a Band-Aid, sticking meaningless cliches over a raw, gaping wound. The scars of grief remain with us throughout our life.

These women, they loved Jesus, and they'd watched him die. Suffering dreadfully. Suffering shamefully. And when we mourn the loss of a loved one, a friend, we're reminded of the ugliness of death. Death is indeed disgusting. Death is wicked. Because of this reality, that death really is horrible, we don't give empty, Christian platitudes. We won't "make it better" if we just say the right thing, will we?

No. Instead, we gather our beloved brother or sister in our arms, and we mourn with them. Their pain is real. Their loneliness is real. Their emptiness is real. And what is vital to understand is that we don't deny them this. Grief is important. To grieve is to acknowledge the loss. To accept the pain of the loss. It is to express the anger at the Fall which made the loss possible, and, ultimately, inevitable. Jesus understood this anger when he stood at the tomb of Lazarus and screamed in rage.

But although we permit grief, and although we share in grief, we do not succumb to grief. We know that death is defeated but it remains to be banished. Perhaps you have been to gravesides this past year. I have. And perhaps we will travel there this year. We grieve. We grieve the loss. But we do not bend to the death. We are not overcome. Because we know, we *know*, that Christ has conquered. Death is *not* the end. Death does *not* have the last word.

Because death is *not* the end. Even as we watch our loved ones die, and our loved ones grieve, we mourn differently. We mourn with hope and with confidence. As painful as the separation is here and now, there is joy and hope in eternity with Christ.

And that is *not* a cliché. If Christ remained dead? Then yes, death is victorious, and we have nothing. No hope. No peace. No comfort.

But if Christ *truly* is the king, then he brings with his resurrection a confidence even in the midst of the pain and angst of grief and death. We must never treat the resurrection life and hope that Christ gives to us as a cliché. It is the surest, deepest, truth, and reality. It's a very real, deep, heart-impacting truth: The sting of death *is defeated* by the power that raised Christ from the grave. And as Paul reminds us, the sting of death is sin; and the strength of sin is the Law.

But!

Thanks be to God, for we have been given *victory* through our Lord Jesus Christ.

It isn't vapidity to point to the resurrection; it's certainty. It's pointing to the promises of the only one who has bested that old evil enemy of death. It's trusting in the one who was swallowed by the grave and in doing so swallowed *up* the grave. In victory. And so, grieving Christian, remember that God himself knows your pain. He understands grief. He watched as his own Son was killed, ravaged by the evils of the Fall. He knows your anger, sadness, pain. He "gets it." He understands where you are emotionally standing.

And yet.

Just like this angel speaking to the women, Mark points you *away* from loss *to* the grave and *towards* the Lord *over* the grave. It's because of his victory that we have confidence that Christ has achieved salvation not merely *from* sin, but *to* eternal life. This is the gospel reality. And if you *are* reading this with grief on your heart, beloved brother or sister. We weep with you. Our hearts break for you. You are not alone.

But Christ has spoken; and death is defeated. Grieving Christian, take heart; your king comforts you. He knows about death more intimately than even you do in the midst of your pain. Be like these women and lead your grief back to the king, because he *is* the *king*, and he has overcome even that last great enemy of death. This world is fleeting, and those wounds are real, and they will last until your own dying day or Christ's triumphant return. But they *will* end. Christ has promised that there will be a time when death will be no more, when our tears of grief will be washed away.

Dear brother. Dear sister. Persevere. Keep your eyes fixed on Christ, and he *will* bring you through. Even through this lonely tunnel of grief. Because Christ was raised to life again.

And what did that resurrection achieve?

Everything! The resurrection proves that the Jesus of the gospels is different the Jesuses presented to us by the world.

Unlike the world's Jesuses, he's not merely a genie in a lamp to make us rich.

He's not simply a therapist to fix your problems.
He's not simply a prayer prayed to get out of Hell free.
He's not simply an SOS when times are tough.
He's not simply a counsellor to fix your relationships.
He's the *king*.

And because of the resurrection, all our injustice, all our pain, all our persecution, all our heartache, all our sickness, all our grieving, all our sadness, all our tears, all of it *will* be dealt with.

Because of the resurrection, justice is satisfied. God's promises are kept. Propitiation is made. Prophecies are fulfilled. Reconciliation is possible. Imputation is made visible. Justification by faith is reality. Because of the resurrection, the cosmos is turned upside down. Because of the resurrection Sin was subjected to him. The Fall was repealed by him. Shame was ruined by him. Suffering was sweetened by him.   Disease was destroyed by him. Demons were conquered by him. Death was defeated by him. God's wrath was satisfied by him. Justice was delivered by him. Creation was renewed by him. Salvation was achieved by him. Atonement was completed by him. Regeneration was brought by him. Propitiation was made by him. Reconciliation was attained by him. Justification was declared by him.   Adoption was accomplished by him. Union with God was provided by him. Sanctification is possible because of him. Forgiveness was given by him. His return was guaranteed by him. Resurrection was promised by him. Eternity was granted by him.

Every spiritual promise was fulfilled in, and by, and through Jesus of Nazareth, because of his faithful, sinless obedience, to the Father. And we get access to it all, to him, through faith in him. Because of the resurrection. This is what the king achieved. The battle has been won, the kingdom has been inaugurated, and the authority of the king is established forevermore. Just as God promised.

His throne is eternal.
His reign is just.
His might is transcendent.
His glory is inexorable.
His return is inevitable.

And his march continues in victory, now and to the end of the age. He was, is, and forever will be, the king. This is the resurrection life applied to you and to me. This is the power that takes us through each difficult week. This is the resurrection power that, by his Spirit, indwells every single believer.

The same Spirit that raised *him* from the dead can help *you* put the device down when lust calls. The Spirit can aid you to do your own work rather than cheat. The Spirit can give you the words to say in difficult moments. The Spirit can carry you when you feel broken and bruised. The Spirit will intercede for you when you can't find your voice.

Preaching pastors. Elders. Deacons. Teachers. Church Members. Professors in seminary. This is the *source* of our victorious Christian living; not in our *will*, not in our *effort*, not in our *strength*, but in the *resurrection power* which has been *given* to us by our resurrected Lord.

And that changes everything.

Beloved. Bruised though you may feel; raise your weary head. Look to the cross and see your salvation and freedom. Look to the empty tomb and see your future and your hope. And then lift your tired feet and keep on marching for the king. Wherever he has placed you, right now, is where he wants you to be. Live for him there. Speak for him there. Cling to him there. Be faithful to him there.

He will never leave you nor forsake you. Because he is alive and lives forevermore. And has sent his Spirit to dwell in you and conform you into his likeness and image.

Aftermath

The guards finally woke up and realized they must report back. A small contingent went to the priests and elders. In a sense, the camera of the gospel narratives panned back to the priests as we're forced to wonder: What would they do with the news of the empty tomb? After all, they had furiously plotted to avoid such a scenario. Their seal had broken, their guards had fainted, and their plot had failed. The logical thing would be to see the empty tomb for what it was: Evidence of the resurrection.

But instead of repenting and believing in Jesus of Nazareth, they remained true to type. Once again, they concocted a plan to deny the resurrection. They bribed the guards, and, after what appears to have bene a bartering session, they fed them a lie. It was a pretty bad one, too. The guards were bribed to say that they had fallen asleep, at which point the disciples had sneakily come to the massive stone, broke the wax seal, *moved* the boulder, nicked the body, and made off with it without rousing them. If such a story were true, *they* must have had the sleep of the *dead*. This concocted story wouldn't stand up to the mildest of cross-examination: If they'd been asleep, how do they know who stole the body? How deep must their sleep have been for them not to hear the massive stone being rolled away?

But this was to be their story. As part of their negotiation with the Chief Priests, they were able to extract a promise from the priests that they could rely on them to provide defense in case Pilate found out about their lie and demanded that they be killed for their supposed lapse. Their fear was legitimate: In Roman military culture, a sentry found asleep was to be executed to serve as a warning that jeopardizing the troop was a serious breach of loyalty and responsibility.

This lie they perpetuated? It continued even into the second and third century. But it doesn't matter, does it?

It doesn't matter what the priests planned. Jesus is alive.

It doesn't matter what the soldiers said. Jesus is alive.
It doesn't matter what Thomas Jefferson taught. Jesus is alive.
It doesn't matter what society tells you to think. Jesus is alive.

The truth is out. Jesus is alive. And the lie can't change it. No matter what they say. No matter what people choose to believe. The truth is the truth. And because Jesus is alive?

The march of the king continues.

Chapter Four:

...Because of the Ascension

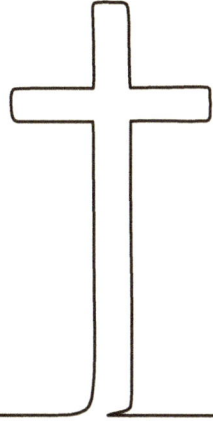

[Luke 24:51] *While He blessed them, He parted from them, and was carried up into heaven.*

Introduction

Do you remember the last time you said goodbye?

I remember saying goodbye to friends and family about 11 years ago, boarding a big plane, and moving halfway across the world. And it was a fun adventure to be sure. But it was daunting.

And yet, from my perspective, I was moving onto something new and exciting. But the people I'd grown up with and gone to school with and skipped college classes with and shared life with? I was leaving *them* behind as well.

They were no longer *there* in my day-to-day experience. Granted, with technology, things were easier than in previous generations. In our modern world we can communicate via video chat and instant communication and so on, and that certainly made, and makes, it easier. But the reality continues to be that I'm here. And they're not.

Very recently, we dropped my visiting nephews back to the airport. And we watched as planes rose up and flew away, taking them back to Ireland and away from us. Every visit feels too short, and every interregnum feels much too long.

But there's something about *that* image, isn't there? The image of a plane taxiing out, taking off, gaining altitude, and then flying away is very powerful. It's a poignant image for many. In fact, it's become something of a trope in TV shows, hasn't it? Typically characters who realize *quite* late that they really *do* love the guy or girl who's about to leave. And the camera follows the lovelorn desperados as they race to get to the airport, very magically making it through security (which anyone who's ever flown in the last 20 years knows is simply not happening!), and then arriving at their departure gate in a flurry of desperation and excitement. The stress and the drama of trying to hurry through the cavernous maze of the marble white airport to find the person they love is powerfully conveyed with the aid of tension-building music and cinematography. And, if it's a dramatic TV show, the lover will *just c*atch them at the gate. But if it's a *really* dramatic show, the lover will just *miss* them at the gate! (Which begs the question why *they* don't have cell phones and just call one another...) But for those who miss one another, we hear the sad music pick up as we watch them gazing forlornly at the plane through the hazy window as it moves away from the gate and taxis to the runway and then...poof. It flies away. In cinema, this is called the *pathos* moment. The *all is lost* moment. And it's meant to feel emotional and traumatic. And it's dramatic because the script makes it all *feel* so *final*.

If you're of an older generation, perhaps the plane image isn't one that captivates you quite so much as others. But there are iconic pictures of soldiers boarding ships in America and heading to Europe to fight the Nazis. Such images show women standing along the hull of the vast ship and throwing flowers and kisses towards their beloved as tears stream down their face. And the reality was sharp: They didn't know if *their* man would return. Yes, the duty was glorious, and the fight was moral, and the job was necessary, but it was nevertheless extremely unnerving for all concerned. But it was a different kind of sadness and fear for those who were left behind. To live life *without* their beloved.

Whether it's a plane or a ship or car or even a bicycle, the idea of someone leaving to go elsewhere is always difficult for those who love them but remain. Mothers worry about their distant children. Friends miss the community that had been fostered over shared experiences and, most likely, mischievous activities that parents don't know about. The adventurer feels that sense of absence also, of course; but it's the ones at home, who don't have the excitement of the *new*. They remain in the doldrums of the humdrum daily life as it was *but without you*; they feel the absence most keenly.

In this chapter, we're going to consider another very surprising and dramatic "goodbye." And it certainly felt final to the disciples of Jesus. And although Jesus had left them, it was the disciples who returned to life that, although everything had *changed*? Their life, in many ways remained very similar. Daily chores still needed accomplished, familiar tensions and problems existed; indeed, in some cases, life actually *grew much worse* for those left behind. They had the humdrum, the boring, side of things, whilst Jesus? His exaltation was very different! He was in a very different circumstance. But the disciples, newly commissioned as the apostles, had to keep going. Only now they had to keep going without Jesus physically present to guide and teach them. And the question they had was simple: How? How do we accomplish this mission without Jesus here?

But we're also going to see in this chapter that it was not a *final* goodbye. *Jesus'* goodbye has a very different ending. There's a different kind of 'hope' expressed in Jesus' goodbye and absence. Things *are* different; but there's no uncertainty and no lack of confidence about what Jesus has promised and therefore what he *will* do.

We come now to the point where we'll consider the amazing moment when Jesus of Nazareth, the *resurrected* Jesus of Nazareth, *ascended* back to heaven from which he had first come. Our source for this event is the author Luke. He wrote both the *Gospel According to Luke* and the *Acts of the Apostles*. In writing these two books, he was trying to give a forensic, historical account of the life of Jesus and the expansion of the early church to Theophilis. There's some debate as to whether or not Theophilis was a real person. This is because the name *Theophilis* means 'lover of God' and therefore it could be that Luke wrote the biography of Jesus and the history of the early church as a means to support and encourage every 'lover of God'; but it could equally be an individual to whom Luke was specifically writing. For our purposes, it doesn't particularly matter. However, we who love God should read Luke's account and be encouraged in our love for our glorious God and his wondrous work of salvation.

The first account of the ascension is found at the end of Luke's first book, his account of the life and ministry of Jesus. He repeats it at the start of his second book, the *Acts of the Apostles*. We will explore his account in his gospel as it contains slightly more information.

[Luke 24:50] *Then He led them out as far as Bethany, and lifting up His hands He blessed them.*

[51] *While He blessed them, He parted from them, and was carried up into heaven.*

[52] *And they worshipped Him and returned to Jerusalem with great joy,*

[53] *and were continually in the temple blessing God.*

Context

We return to the experience of the disciples. And they are absolutely *gobsmacked!* The last few years of their lives had been absolutely crazy. They had walked with Jesus and watched him heal the sick, free the oppressed, and raise the dead. They had heard his incredible teaching and glimpsed the majesty of God. In fact, they had even *done* amazing things themselves as they had received his power as his ambassadors.

But the last two months had been much more challenging. They had seen Jesus be arrested and convicted in a kangaroo court. They had watched him be tortured. They had witness him die. In humiliation. Abused. Abased. Bruised. Broken.

Jesus had been dead.

But since the resurrection they knew that he was *alive*. For *forty* whole days they had met with him, witnessed him, heard him, touched him, beheld him, and marveled at him. And then they made their way to Bethany where Jesus started to bless them. It likely took a little time as no doubt there would have been excited discussions and emotional reflections. They nevertheless probably felt something unique was happening.

Then, as they watched him, even as they were listening to him as he blessed them? He began to rise from the ground. He wasn't levitating like some kind of tawdry magic trick. He was rising. And they soon had to crane their necks as they tried to keep their eyes on him. But he kept rising.

He eventually rose into the heavens and out of sight. And they stood staring with their mouths agape in confusion and surprise. It was certainly quite the goodbye. Hollywood TV shows in airports have little on *this* kind of departure.

The Risen Lord Is the Reigning Lord

This is an incredible account. It's okay to acknowledge that. No doubt the disciples were just as amazed at that moment as we are when we read their account about it. But this is not the only unique time in the ministry of Jesus where specifically incredible events take place on a mountain top.

You may remember in Matthew's account of the life of Jesus that he had taken a few of his disciples up Mount Tabor before Holy Week. Suddenly, the disciples who had journeyed with him up to the peak saw that they were joined by two new figures. They soon realized that these two men were the very important prophets from the Old Testament: Moses and Elijah. Together, they symbolized the Law (of Moses) and the Prophets (the rest of the Old Testament). 'Moses' and 'Elijah' were used as shorthand phrases that encapsulated the entire corpus of their work in much the same way we use 'gospel' to mean the entire work of Jesus.

But on Mount Tabor, during the transfiguration, something special occurred. Even as Jesus was conversing with Moses and Elijah, who symbolized the major authors of the Mosaic covenant and Israel's failure to be obedient, a voice from heaven penetrated the skies and declared: "This is my beloved Son with whom I am well pleased. Listen to him" (Matthew 17:5). That last little phrase is extremely important theologically. In Deuteronomy, many centuries earlier, Moses had written that Israel was to expect another prophet like Moses. This passage is worth reading:

> [Deuteronomy 18:15] *"The LORD your God will raise up for you a prophet like me [Moses] from among you, from your brothers—it is to him you shall listen—*
>
> [16] *just as you desired of the LORD your God at Horeb on the day of the assembly, when you said, 'Let me not hear again the voice of the LORD my God or see this great fire any more, lest I die.'*
>
> [17] *And the LORD said to me, 'They are right in what they have spoken.*
>
> [18] *I will raise up for them a prophet like you from among their brothers. And I will put my words in his mouth, and he shall speak to them all that I command him.*
>
> [19] *And whoever will not listen to my words that he shall speak in my name, I myself will require it of him.*

On Mount Tabor, then, Deuteronomy 18 was being fulfilled by Jesus. The new prophet *that Moses had said would come* had finally arrived. The greater Moses with a greater covenant had come. He would not only *speak* the words of God; he would *be* the *Word* made flesh, as we saw in chapter 1. It's not insignificant that this proclamation in Matthew 17 came after a period of Jesus' ministry in which he performed miracles reminiscent of those God had performed for Israel as recorded in the book of Exodus. What was incredibly difficult for the Israelites of Jesus' day was not that he was performing these "Exodus-miracles" but that he was *including* Gentiles in them, such as the feedings in the wilderness (Matthew 14:13-21 and Matthew 15:32-39), walking on the water, and his use of the divine name (Matthew 14:22-33). During this section of Matthew's gospel, Jesus had also been attacking the legalism and faux religiosity of the Jewish religious elite and leaders by correctly interpreting Moses and revealing the spiritual bankruptcy of those leaders (Matthew 15:1-20 and Matthew 16:1-12). Not only were these events making the significant point that Jesus was, in a sense, "doing Moses," but differently; but Matthew seems to be making that point that Jesus was doing Moses *indiscriminately*: He healed the sick at Gennesaret (Matthew 14:34-36), and praised the faith of a Canaanite woman in direct contrast to the Pharisees who cared only for legalism and who demanded signs before believing (Matthew 15:21-28).

Understanding that these things were placed together helps explain the true significance of the Mount of Transfiguration. Immediately after those events and lessons, Peter incredibly declared that Jesus is the Son of the living God, God's Anointed One (Matthew 16:16) and Jesus told them that he would die and rise again (Matthew 16:21-23). Using similar language, he told them that they must take up their cross (the implement of death and treason in their world) and follow him (meaning, by implication, to follow Christ in dying to the world).

This is the *astounding* context to the Mount of Transfiguration. There, then, as we have seen, Jesus was joined with Moses and Elijah, the symbols of all the Old Testament Israelite world and its covenantal structure of temple worship, sacrifice, and wicked religious elite. And the voice of heaven called out and demanded that the disciples listen to...who? Moses the Law-giver? Moses the leader who led the nascent nation out of Egypt? Or Elijah the chief of the Old Testament prophets? Elijah who had faced Ba'al's prophets and rebuked wicked kings?

No. They're to listen to *his Son*, with whom God the Father is well pleased. This teaches us that the Old Covenant? The law and the prophets? They were *giving way* to Jesus. A new era was dawning. A greater Moses and a greater prophet had come. And he is not simply *another* law-giver nor another prophetic voice in the wilderness; he is something bigger, vaster, grander, greater, and more powerful. And, therefore, what *he* inaugurates is going to be greater than what had come before.

God the Father had spoken at that moment and told the disciples that Jesus was the fulfilment of the promise given *by* Moses that another prophet like Moses would come. This implies that this new prophet was to be a leader of a new nation, rescued from the wickedness of slavery to a dictatorial ruler of evil. And on Mt. Tabor, God declared that was being fulfilled in their presence and *God himself* proclaimed that *Jesus* was this promised one. They were to listen to him; the Old Covenant would soon be abrogated by the cross of Christ. The cross would fulfil the Old Covenant. And something new was dawning before their eyes.

Is it any wonder they were gobsmacked when Jesus, on the Mount of Olives, began to ascend into the heavens? Their knowledge that he was God was being reinforced yet again. And that was, no doubt, exhilarating.

And yet.

Blessed Them and Left Them

Jesus was *ascending* into the heavens. He was *leaving* them. Their task was now going to be so much more difficult. After all, had Jesus remained? Well, he couldn't die (or at least stay dead). They could go into every nation and bring Jesus with them as evidence for their claims. Without him, however, it would be more difficult. And no doubt the magnitude of their task was beginning to hit them as they wondered about the logistics.

It's important to remember that we know from John's account that Jesus had warned them this would happen. He had quite specifically stated that he would ascend and return to his Father in heaven (we will return to this section of John's account below).

Thus, they watched amazed, bamboozled, and gobsmacked, as the *resurrected* Lord once again rose. Not from the grave though; this time from the *earth* itself. And ascended into heaven.

Went Into Heaven

There's quite a bit to unpack here, theologically. But firstly, let's remember that Jesus is *still* incarnate. He's certainly God the eternal Son, but he's also *still* the *incarnate* Son of God. Jesus is God-made-flesh, even in the resurrection. Therefore, the ascending Jesus is no phantom or Casper the Friendly Ghost. This is *Jesus*, the resurrected Lord. And he *bodily*, *visibly*, and *physically* ascended. (That point is important – hold that in your cap for now.)

But he also ascended *to somewhere*: To a Place. He went into *the heavens* to the Father. Consider, now, what Hebrews 1 says:

[Hebrews 1:2] *but in these last days God has spoken to us by His Son, whom He appointed the heir of all things, through whom also He created the world.*

[3] *He is the radiance of the glory of God and the exact imprint of His nature, and He upholds the universe by the word of His power. After making purification for sins, He sat down at the right hand of the Majesty on High.*

These verses tell us that Jesus *physically* ascended to heaven *where he was seated* at the right hand of the Father. What does this mean?

Well, you *may* remember all the way back in Genesis, after God had created everything, that on the seventh day, he *rested*. Now that doesn't mean that God was *tired* and took a nap on His heavenly E-Z BOY. No, of course not. It means that the work was *finished*. God's work of creation had been completed; everything he had desired to make had been created and placed where it needed to be. The work had been accomplished. And God rested.

I recently built a filing cabinet in my office. It wasn't particularly complicated, but I nevertheless completed it with relatively few errors. After I'd finished building it, however, I took a seat. Why? Because the job, the task, was over. I didn't need to do any more tinkering. There was a sense of satisfaction at the task's completion. I could rest from the labor; I wasn't *tired*, but I was *finished*. We see this from Christ on the cross, also. Some of Jesus' last words were simply "it is finished!"

Thus, at the ascension, Jesus returned to heaven because he had *completed his mission*. The work was finished. And the conquering king, the Word-made-flesh, the resurrected lord, took his rightful seat with the Father.

What was this work that was now completed? Hebrews explains that he "made purification for sins." This tells us that his death on the cross was successful. His work of dying in the place of mankind and bearing the punishment for sin had been completed. And it further explains that the resurrection to bring new creation life for his people was successful. And *now* it was to be implemented. This is why Jesus takes his place on his rightful throne from which he will *reign* as the resurrected Lord.

✝ Application: Tumultuous Times

Perhaps you've been watching the news recently? We live in tumultuous times, don't we? Wars in the Middle East and in Europe are still ongoing. There's been chaos in global trade, with possibly a cold trading war that may well lead to proxy, even hot, wars between the superpowers. It can feel like the world is going to hell in handcart. We can often fall prey to despair about the world and the future.

Christian. Remember that Christ is risen. And Christ *is* reigning.

Maybe you've watched the madness of the stocks and bonds markets and are worried about your pensions, your savings, or your retirement future. You're worried about the rate of inflation and the potential costs of products rising as tariffs are being floated across the board?

Christian. Remember that Christ is risen. And Christ is reigning.

Maybe you've received a troubling diagnosis. Perhaps your relationship is on the rocks. It could be the case that your children are wayward. Debts can run high. Poor decisions can have disastrous results. Things beyond our control can nevertheless affect us and hurt us.

Christian. Remember that Christ is risen. And Christ is reigning.

Each of us knows what it's like to be in a fierce battle with temptation and sin. You know what you *ought to do*, what it means for you to die to self and take up your cross and follow Christ. But there are days when you lack the courage and human willpower while sin's pull feels so seductive and strong.

Christian. Remember that Christ is risen. And Christ is reigning.

Whether it's your personal situations or the global geopolitics across the world, Christ is *still* sovereign. He is risen from the dead. And he *is* reigning from his throne. He has completed his work of redemption. He has completed your salvation. His blood has achieved your forgiveness. The resurrection has brought about the New Creation. The New Creation *has* begun. And therefore, even when your life, or our world, looks and feels and sounds topsy-turvy and frightening, we're called to remember that Christ is risen and Christ is reigning. He is risen from the dead and is seated in the throne room of heaven. Because the work has been accomplished: It is finished.

What does that mean for us? It means that we have an advocate *in the most powerful situation room in the cosmos.* We have an elder brother, through adoption, who quite literally *died to save us.* He has promised us that he will help us, hear us, and advocate for us. This means, Christian, that you pray to a *listening* Lord. You ask, Christian, from a *generous* king. You worship, Christian, a *worthy* God. Not a corpse. Not a myth. Not a mystery. Not a liar. Not a lunatic. Not a loser. Not a legend.

A *risen* and *reigning* Lord.

This is why the disciples went away worshipping, isn't it? Because it could certainly be traumatizing for them to realize that their Lord has ascended and *left them behind.* But they were beginning to see the bigger picture. They understood that if Christ truly *is* risen. Then death? It has no true power. Its sting is defeated, as Paul reminds us in 1 Corinthians 15:55. And if Christ is *reigning*? Then this world holds nothing to fear: Christ is in charge. That doesn't mean it will always be *easy* or go exactly however *we* want. We know that many of these same, worshipping, apostles, would ultimately give their lives in observance of Christ's commission. But this world holds less fear and less power over us when we remember that Christ is in charge.

It doesn't matter if Red or Blue is in the White House: Christ rules from the heavenly house. Do you hear that? Do you believe that? Has your conversation and your life reflected that in the last four weeks? How about the last 4 years? When 'your side' isn't in power, do your words, do your actions, does your faith reflect an unwavering acceptance that God is in control? That Christ is reigning? Or are you fickle and blown about by the winds of earthly change? Are we content to rest in the reality of Psalm 2, where we read that God scoffs at the wicked plans of rogue rulers and petty kings? Why does God mock them? Because he promised the Psalmist that he would "set his King on Zion, his holy hill...and make the nations his heritage and the ends of the earth his possession" (Psalm 2:7-8). This has now been accomplished by the exaltation of Jesus Christ. God's king reigns from heaven's throne.

Christ is risen.

Christ is reigning.

Because the work has been completed.

And this was why the disciples could worship.

...But Jesus Was Gone

But.

The reality was the case. Back in Jerusalem, even as they gathered and worshipped in the temple portico, they had to come to terms with their reality: Jesus *was* gone. He had ascended. He *had* left. They were bereft. The Lord was gone.

And, no doubt, some of them remembered Jesus' words in the Great Commission. He had told them that he'd *never leave* them or forsake them. Yet now he *was* gone.

Yes, the reigning Lord is the risen Lord. But he's also, *in a sense,* an *absent* Lord. At least, I'm sure, that's how it *felt.*

So what's going on?

Well, a little more theology will help us figure it out.

The Reigning Lord is the Sending Lord

[John 16:4b] *"I did not say these things to you from the beginning, because I was with you.*

[5] But now I am going to Him who sent me, and none of you asks me, 'Where are you going?'

[6] But because I have said these things to you, sorrow has filled your heart.

[7] Nevertheless, I tell you the truth: it is to your advantage that I go away...

We move from Luke's account to John's biography of Jesus. These verses are before the crucifixion, when the disciples were still struggling to understand what exactly was going on. It's a continual surprise to read the gospels and to see repeatedly that, despite how explicit Jesus was about his death and resurrection, the disciples seemed cloth-eared. This was one such moment.

It's Better That I Leave

We're jumping into a conversation Jesus was having with his confused disciples. You can see, in verse 5, that Jesus was clear: "I'm going to go away. And I'm going to back to my Father. To the One who sent me."

We've just seen that fulfilled in Luke 24. This means that Jesus had told them to anticipate the ascension. They *had been told it would happen.* But then Jesus went one step further. In verse 7, he explicitly stated: "It's *to your advantage that I go away."*

Say what?!

It's at this point that I reckon there would have been quite a bit of confusion amongst the disciples. Prior to the resurrection, it might have appeared intimidating to think of life without their rabbi. But after the resurrection, to say that it would *be better* for them that he would be gone? You can imagine their exasperated confusion.

"Jesus, you're the *risen, reigning* Messiah! How *on earth* (pardon the pun) could it be better that you leave us and go elsewhere? You *literally* defeat death. Let's go fight those nasty pagan Romans. Let's rule the world? Right?!"

Wrong!

Jesus was clear.

It's Better He Leaves

He said that it is better *for them* that he leave them. This can appear quite confusing to us as well as to the disciples, but let's walk through it.

Jesus is *God*. He's God the Son. That means he's divine. He is all powerful. Everything that the Father is, in nature, so is the Son. Thus, from eternity past, God the Son was *omnipresent*. That simply means that he was not bound by space. He was everywhere. God the Son was spirit just like God the Father and the Holy Spirit are spirit.

But here's the thing...you and me? *We're human*. And humans *are* bound by space and time. In other words. You? You can't be here reading this book and *also* at a concert bopping along to your favorite band. Humans can't be in two places at once. It's a defining characteristic of being made of matter, skin and bones: Flesh. To be a human is to be bound by the laws of physics.

This means that God the *Son*? He's *different* than you and me. He is spirit. He is omnipresent.

But remember chapter 1? God the Son? *Becomes* the son of Mary. The *omnipresent* Son becomes the *unipresent* son. He becomes the son, *present* on earth.

This was the word 'incarnate': God-made-flesh.

So what does all this theology teach us?

We're realizing that *because* Jesus remains incarnate and is in the heavenly places, he is seated at the right hand of the Father. And he *remains* the God-man, the Word-made-flesh, incarnate. This means that he remains bound (by his own sovereign choice) by the rules and limitations that he himself created. Thus, although Jesus is God the Son, *because* he is also the Son of Mary and Joseph, truly human, he cannot be in two places at once.

Now, let's think about that. Because this creates a little bit of a theological paradox for us. At the Great Commission in Matthew 28, Jesus told his disciples that he would be "with you until the end of the age." But, in John 16, he told them he would leave them, return to the Father, and that his absence would be better for them. Then, in Luke, we read that he ascended to the heavens. And they could not see him anymore.

Did he lie? Had they lost their Lord? After all, humans can't be in two places at one time. And Jesus is now in heaven. They saw him ascend and disappear from view.

The answer to this conundrum is found in John 16.

But I Will Send

> [John 16:7] *Nevertheless, I tell you the truth: it is to your advantage that I go away, for if I do not go away, the Helper will not come to you. But if I go, I will send Him to you.*

Jesus will *send*.

You see the answer to our puzzle is quite simple. If Jesus can only be in one place at a time because he's incarnate? And yet he had promised to be with us until the end of the age? Then something's missing.

And that *something* isn't a *thing*; turns out, he's a Person. In John 16:7, Jesus explained that when his work was finished, he would ascend to his throne beside the Father. And from the throne, he would *send* the *Helper*, the Advocate, the Holy Spirit.

And the Spirit, sometimes called the Holy Ghost in older translations, would teach the disciples to remember all that Jesus had taught and commanded them. Jesus, even as he told them to anticipate the ascension, had at the same time promised to send the Holy Spirit to be with them. This Spirit would come from Jesus who was now in the heavens.

But there's a little more to grasp.

The Holy Spirit is *omnipresent* because he is the third Person of the one Godhead. This means that the Spirit of Christ, the Spirit of God, the Holy Spirit, is truly God in all his attributes, including that he is, very obviously, spirit. As such, therefore, the Holy Spirit is everywhere; he is *not* defined or contained by space like the incarnate Son. This is partly why Jesus said that it would be better for the apostles that he would ascend. Their situation wouldn't be better because Jesus would be *absent* but because the Holy Spirit would be *present*. And the Spirit is not bound by space or limited by geography. Which means that even when the apostles split up to preach the gospel to very different locations such as west to Rome and east to India, the Spirit of Christ *would be with them*. This is why the ascension would lead to Pentecost. Jesus had ascended; now they had to await the arrival of the promised Helper.

When we return, now to Luke's accounts, this time to the Acts of the Apostles, we read the following:

[Acts 2:1] *When the day of Pentecost arrived, they were all together in one place.*

[2] *And suddenly there came from heaven a sound like a mighty rushing wind, and it filled the entire house where they were sitting.*

[3] *And divided tongues as of fire appeared to them and rested on each one of them.*

[4] *And they were all* filled with the Holy Spirit.

He Sends the Spirit

At Pentecost the Holy Spirit *did* come to the Apostles. And when he came upon them as tongues of fire, he fulfilled Jesus' promise to teach the disciples to remember all that Jesus had taught them, and *this* also fulfilled the New Covenant prophecies in Jeremiah 31 and Ezekiel 36 and 37. Their hearts of stone and confusion about the gospel were transformed into hearts of belief and of true flesh. No longer were they hardened or dulled to the true message of God's messiah, but instead they could truly believe and obey. Their souls which were dead in sin were now resurrected by the power of the same Holy Spirit who raised Christ from the dead. Their hearts were circumcised through faith to *know* and *believe* the gospel that Christ died and rose again to save sinners.

But it gets even better.

Just as Jesus had 'done Moses' and included the Gentiles? Well, *incredibly*, the coming of the Spirit is *also* told in Acts 10, but there the Spirit descended on not on Jews, but on *Gentiles*. And that is hugely significant because it tells us that the gospel of Jesus's life, death, and resurrection is for *anyone who will believe*. Unlike the Old Covenant under the Law and the Prophets (symbolized by Moses and Elijah), where outsiders could only return to the one, true, God *through* Israel, now we see that *anyone* can return to the one, true, God through the one, true, *Israelite*: Jesus of Nazareth, who *is* the one, true, God. And anyone who believes in Christ will be reconciled to God by having their sins forgiven and being filled with the Holy Spirit who will circumcise their heart and raise their spiritually dead soul to spiritual and eternal life.

Immediately.

The primary purpose of the Spirit's ministry, then, is *not* to be filled *so that you speak in tongues* or do miracles, but that the Spirit of God *lives* within you. The point of Acts 2 and Acts 10 is that the Spirit of God resides within *every* true believer of Christ. That includes *you* if you are a Christian.

The Spirit lives in you to help you do what? As Jesus promised in John 16, his ministry is to teach you about what it means to follow Christ and to be a citizen of Christ's glorious kingdom.

And each one of us needs this, don't we? Because, dear friend, the Christian life is not a hobby. It's not a 'come to church two times a year to doff your cap to God' and think you're now best buds with him. The Christian life is not something that you can subscribe to by paying a little tithe occasionally and you're good, you're in, now God owes you the product of salvation.

To be a Christian is to be *invaded, indwelt,* and *enabled* by the Holy Spirit who will teach you how to look and sound and live like Christ.

When I'm teaching about this to my wonderful college students, I have a picture of a Dickensian scene in my mind. I think of it as coming from that marvelous scene towards the end of *A Christmas Carol* where Scrooge finally accepts his nephew's invitation to come and dine with his family. The Christian life is a little like this. Imagine, if you will, a very grand lord's house at dinnertime. There's a glorious feast of chicken, beef, and all kinds of carbs and veggies. And outside, looking in, is a scruffy, unkept, dirty, little street urchin (or Uncle Scrooge, if you prefer). The orphan is starving and he looks longingly at the food on the table. But he's not welcome. He's not a member of the family.

But then something incredible happens. The door opens and the master of the house speaks with the snot-nosed, filthy child and not only *invites* him to dine, but actually *adopts* the boy into his family. Now, suddenly, everything has changed. He has *every right* to be there. He has *become* part of the family, hasn't he? He can sit at the table and enjoy all the food and blessings that the master, his now-*father*, offers to him. That's the glory of our adoption in Christ. We are now part of God's family.

However, there's something else going. You see, because the orphan has gained a father, he is now a *son*. And that comes not only with *blessing,* but *responsibility*. The child *has been* adopted. That isn't going to change. But now, *as a consequence* of his adoption, he has to *wear* and *bear* the family name. He can't eat dinner and then go out and live on the streets again. He has a home. And so, as *part* of his new sonship, he has to learn how to be a family member: Which forks should he use for which dishes, which spoon is for soup and which for dessert, how to talk across the table at a guest. He must learn the manners, the rules, the etiquettes, of his new family so that he reflects well on his father and siblings.

He's been adopted. Now he gets the *privilege* of looking and sounding and living and loving as one of the family. The Bible calls this 'holiness' and the process of this change is called 'sanctification'. God calls us to be holy as he is holy and provides himself, through the Spirit, to aid us in being transformed into the family likeness. And that can certainly be a jarring experience. But this is the beauty of the work of the Holy Spirit in every single believer's life. He works in each one of us, at our own pace, revealing as much of God's incredible patience and love and grace as we need, as we start to be conformed into the likeness and image of Christ.

This is the work of the Holy Spirit. For *every single believer.*

Do you hear that, Christian? It's for you. This work is happening to you. Even now. In this moment, the Spirit is teaching you about the words and commands of Jesus as you read this chapter and reflect on what it means to be a Christian.

Think, then, what this means for us in our lives. The Holy Spirit, who is the Third Person of the Trinity, is the Spirit of the Father. And he's also the Spirit of the Son. Which means that he *represents* Christ to us every moment of every day. Because he is the Spirit of the Son, and the Godhead is one being, one God, in three persons, we can say that Jesus *is* with us and will never leave us nor forsake us, even to the end of the age.

Further, this means that we have the *power* of God Most High residing in us. He empowers us to be obedient like Christ. He enables us to be a godly believer. He transforms us into conformity with our elder brother. We are, with every moment of the Spirit's work in us, becoming more and more like Jesus. From the marble of our dead bodies, the Holy Spirit is chiseling something majestic and beautiful: Living souls who live and love like the Lord Jesus.

✟ Application: The Spirit at Work in Us

Thus, when those moments of temptation come, we *do* have the (spiritual) strength to overcome. It isn't the strength of our willpower, but the strength to submit to Christ's Spirit and let him empower us to resist.

When the colleague at work is flirting with you? Hear the teaching of the Spirit: Do not commit adultery.

When the temptation to lie comes towards you? Hear the teaching of the Spirit: Do not lie.

When the temptation of anxiety, worry, doubt, or fear threatens to overwhelm you? You pray to a Risen and reigning Lord, and he has sent his Holy Spirit to *reside* in you, to aid you, teach you, to help you, to shape you, to mold you.

Listen to him.

Follow him.

When the temptation to compromise your holiness, your witness, your faith comes? Be it through your boss, the government, your spouse, your friendship group, your boyfriend/girlfriend? You have the Spirit of God who raised Christ from the dead dwelling in you. You *can* persevere and reject sin *through his power at work in you*.

Christian, this means that you *can* fight sin. The Spirit of Christ enables and empowers you. The question is not *can you*, but *will* you? Will you rely on the Spirit's strength? Or will you rest on your own efforts and falter and stumble?

But if you're *not* yet submitting to the risen, reigning Lord? Then I'm afraid the Spirit of Christ is *not* in you. He isn't residing in you, nor is he enabling you to fight sin. In fact, Scripture tells you that rather than being *free* in Christ? You are *enslaved* to darkness. Rather than belonging to Christ, you are serving the prince and the power of the air. You are in chains to sinfulness, to shame, to Satan himself, and will share in his eternal destiny.

The Bible tells us that those who are not in Christ are "slaves to sin" (John 8:34; Romans 6:16), That's what you are. And you might buck at reading that and resist that idea. But humor me with an experiment: Try to overcome your sinful desires. Try to stop sinning for a single day. And you'll realize very quickly that, yes, the Bible is right.

But here's the wondrous thing, dear friend. You *don't have to be* enslaved so sin. This is what we've been celebrating in this book. *Because of Jesus*, you don't have to be enslaved to sin and headed for Hell.

Because God the Son, the eternal, majestic, omnipresent Son, became flesh. And, as the God-man, he literally and physically died the most heinous, brutal death at the hands of man, under the judgement of God. He died in our place to pay the debt for our sin.

And then three days later he rose from the dead to conquer the consequences of our rebelliousness, our sinfulness, our hostility, our wickedness. And through his resurrection he brought us the new life and a new hope. The new creation for which our souls have been longing.

God offers this truth, this freedom, this salvation, to you if you receive this message and then accept it by faith and repentance. That means three things: It means acknowledging that you're a sinner. As we've seen, to be a sinner is to be at war with God, hating God, because we want to be God instead. We must acknowledge that is our reality.

Secondly, it means realizing that you can't make amends for your sin. You're guilty. When we admit that we're sinful against a holy, and infinite, God, we are also admitting that we can do nothing in our own efforts to make amends for that debt. We cannot bridge the gap or pay the debt. We're helpless. We need God.

Thus, thirdly, we *accept* the incredible and merciful offer of rec-onciliation, of forgiveness and restoration, of salvation, that Christ has won for us and offered to us. This means that we turn from self-worship and turn towards worshipping the only one worthy of our worship: God. It means refusing sin and choosing Christ. And trusting him. Cling to his sovereign promise that he will save you and will send his Spirit to indwell you and change you and empower you. You will never be the same ever again. And that's a wondrous thing. Instead, you can know that he saves you: Not your work, not your effort, not your attendance, not your money, not your fancy clothes.

Just Jesus. And Jesus alone. He alone can save you.

And he will save you if you cry out to him and ask him. He will not turn you away.

He Sends Us

[Matthew 28:16] *Now the eleven disciples went to Galilee, to the mountain to which Jesus had directed them.*

[17] *And when they saw him they worshipped Him, but some doubted.*

[18] *And Jesus came and said to them, "All authority in heaven and on earth has been given to me.*

[19] *Go therefore and make disciples of all nations, baptizing them in the name of the Father and of the Son and of the Holy Spirit,*

[20] *Teaching them to observe all that I have commanded you. And behold, I am with you always, to the end of the age.*

The Holy Spirit indwells believers and the church. He is the aid and the strength of God to the weary believers who struggle with the trials of the world, the temptations of the flesh, and the terrorizing of the enemy. But he also aids us in obeying the glorious commission of Christ. And because the Holy Spirit is the third Person of the one Godhead, he ensures that Christ is present with us. This is how we obey.

When we think of the Great Commission, we tend to think of the English verb 'go' as the main, or most important, part. But in fact the main point is actually in verse 19 and the start of verse 20. This is because without the *power* of Christ and the *presence* of Christ? We *couldn't obey* the *commission* of Christ. But *because* Christ is all-powerful and has promised his presence (which we now understand is through the indwelling of the Holy Spirit), we *can* be obedient. The promise, therefore, is majestic: "all authority in heaven and on earth" has been given to Jesus.

This giving of authority to Jesus is the fulfilment of many Old Testament passages. We already considered Psalm 2, but consider now Daniel 7:

[Daniel 7:13] *"I saw in the night visions, and behold, with the clouds of heaven there come one like a son of man, and he came to the Ancient of Days and was presented before him.*

[14] *And to him was given dominion, and glory and a kingdom, that all peoples, nations, and languages should serve him; his dominion is an everlasting dominion, which shall not pass away, and his kingdom one that shall not be destroyed."*

The Anointed One, or Messiah, is given the authority of an everlasting kingdom that encompasses all peoples, nations, and languages. This is found in the Great Commission, for the apostles (and through them, we) are sent out to all the world.

In Philippians 2, we see the exaltation of Christ because of his obedience:

[Philippians 2:8] *And being found in human form, he humbled himself by becoming obedient to the point of death, even death on a cross.*

[9] *Therefore, God has highly exalted him and bestowed on him the name that is above every name,*

[10] *so that at the name of Jesus every knee should bow, in heaven and on earth and under the earth,*

[11] *and every tongue confess that Jesus Christ is Lord, to the glory of God the Father.*

The authority that the incarnate Christ now possesses in his triumphant victory is that *all* living creatures will bow before him at the end of all ends and confess that he is truly Lord and God. And, when he returns in might and majesty, he will vanquish the enemies that were defeated at the cross, casting them into the fires of judgement, and hand the kingdom over to the Father, that God will be all in all (1 Corinthians 15:28). What this tells us is that the power, the might, the purposes, the will, and the sovereignty of

God is mediated through the Son. He is the *second* Adam, but he is an infinitely *greater* Adam. God's incarnate Son now bears and utilizes all the divine authority to expand and extend his kingdom until his triumphant return.

Unfortunately, our culture hates Jesus. He's often little more than a cuss word or an insult. Sometimes, he's refashioned into our own image, and so we see the liberal Jesus, the conservative Jesus, the gay Jesus, the Marxist Jesus, the feminist Jesus, the Black Jesus, the white Jesus, the hippy Jesus, and so on. This is not the Jesus of Matthew 28. Sometimes we're offered a weak Jesus, a failed revolutionary Jesus, an inspirational-but-ultimately-useless Jesus. These are not the Jesus of Matthew 28. Jesus is the king. He's risen from the dead. He's reigning on the throne. And he's returning in might and majesty. He is the exalted and all-powerful, anointed Messiah. This is who he is, whether we like it, accept it, believe it, or otherwise. He bears *all* authority in heaven and on earth, and one day all will bow before him and confess his lordship.

Returning to the Great Commission, we are so often taught to focus on the "Go, and make disciples" and apply it, primarily, to missionaries. There is certainly a sense in which it *does* apply to missionaries, of course. But the English translation can be unhelpful here. A stronger translation might be something like: "Therefore, as you are going, making disciples of all nations..." In the Greek, the verb isn't 'go' but 'making disciples.' Therefore, when we consider the Great Commission alongside Jesus' parable in Matthew 22, we can see that it is for *every* believer to obey. As we are going through the highways and byways of our lives, at the crossroads of our daily journeys, we are to be making disciples.

The change in focus of these verses was largely the result of William Carey who helped spur the modern Protestant missionary movement. He helped orient our focus on the idea that we are all *commanded* to 'go' with the gospel. Unfortunately, as so often happens, we tend to overemphasize the 'going' as something specific and foreign rather than daily and routine. But the focus of the command is broader than simply overseas missions. It is for every single Spirit-indwelt disciple.

This means that we, each of us, are to be both evangelists and disciplers, introducing people to the gospel through proclamation as well as teaching people how to live in light of their faith in Christ. If we *truly* believe that Christ is God, and that sin brings death, then we, the church alone, *have the antidote*, the *answer*, the *liftering of freedom* from sin, from death, and from Hell. How much must we *hate* our neighbor, how much must we *hate* our family, how much must we *hate* the person on the street, if we refuse to obey Christ's commission?

We're to be evangelists, sharing the gospel that Christ died for us, bearing our sin and shame and reconciling us to God; that Christ rose again, inaugurating the New Covenant and New Creation; that Christ is reigning, now, over all things; that Christ is returning, to judge the living and the dead.

However, most often you'll hear verse 19 given to missionaries who travel across the world for the kingdom. And that *is* wonderful. It's genuinely truly amazing. And I pray that we raise up missionaries, many missionaries, from the readers of this book. Without a doubt that *is* wonderful.

But Christian, if *that's* what you think is *primarily* going on here? That the Great Commission concerns herculean efforts by the holiest few of Christ's saints? Meanwhile you're consistently sitting in your sweatpants on your recliner? Then you're using foreign missions as an *excuse* for *disobedience*.

Yes, it's true, *some* are called to cross the seas. But, brother and sister, *all* are called to cross the streets. All are called to be making disciples with the gospel. That is a non-negotiable consequence of our being saved and brought into the family of God. We are all to be evangelists in our daily lives.

There is, however, a second aspect to the Great Commission that reflects the Creation Mandate in Genesis. I make this point in greater depth in *"Take and Eat": From Fall To Feast*. But suffice it to say, here, that the Creation Mandate was for the original humanity to procreate (grow in number) and cultivate creation (bringing it under our dominion); the Great Commission is where we evangelize (grow in number) and teach the converts to obey Christ in the New Creation paradigm he has inaugurated (bringing us under Christ's dominion). In both cases, the formula is the same; one earthly and temporal, the second spiritual and eternal: We are to *evangelize* unbelievers. That leads to their *conversion* to faith in Christ. Conversion, in turn, leads to *baptism* in the Triune name. For some, unfortunately, that's considered the end of the journey. You're 'in,' so let's move on and find someone else to evangelize. But that is *not* what Jesus expects of us.

He tells us that when we are converted, we *enter* the kingdom, and then we get baptized. Baptism is like wearing the jersey of Christ's kingdom, as it were. Or, to use our earlier illustration, it's to be adopted into the family of God. But *then* we're to be taught *how to live* and love like Jesus. That is, we're taught to "obey all that He has commanded."

Firstly, in order for us to be obedient to this command, what do we need to be able to teach others? We need to know what Christ has commanded. That's why we need to be *in the word* of God. Reading Scripture. Meditating on it. Digesting it. Reflecting on it. Praying through it and seeking the Holy Spirit's guidance as we do so. And, vitally, following it. So that when we encounter someone who is new in the faith, or, even more excitingly, when we get to lead someone to Christ, we know *how* to obey the *second* half of the Great Commission and help them grow into the likeness of Jesus. And the end goal, of course, is that as a consequence of their discipleship, they, too, can go with Christ and be a disciple-making disciple.

Christian. Are you a Christ-obeying Christian? Are you an evangelist? Are you a discipler? Or do you only provide lip service on a Sunday? I don't know the statistics nationally, but anecdotally, I can say that in the churches I attended, the attendance for

Sunday evening services is dramatically smaller than that of Sunday mornings services. And the prayer meetings are typically the worst attended of all. Leonard Ravenhill famously summed this up with his typical panache: "If you want to know how popular a church is, see Sunday morning. If you want to know how popular the preacher is, go Sunday evening. If you want to know how popular God is, attend the prayer meeting." Are we obedient in our service to Christ because we love our king? Or are we attempting to merely play the game of holiness? Are we simply trying to do enough to get by, to keep God off our backs, and to ensure we get into heaven?

I've often heard complaints that the church service should only last around 60 minutes from start to finish. How on earth are we to be prepared to go into spiritual combat for an entire week, with only 60 minutes' worth of restoring, of rejuvenating, or healing, of training, of discipleship? What other activity in your life would you participate in that would accept that level of commitment? What sport do you think would let you onto the team with a mere 60 minutes of training a week? What orchestra would let you play? What drama team would let you perform? What job would let you out on your own with only 60 minutes' training? What kitchen would let you cook? And yet we think it's okay to treat God with such disinterest and such a limited disregard?

I often challenge my students: Go into your settings on your phone and see what your *daily average* screentime is. Almost *always* it's above five hours. A day. And we resent worshipping with the gathered saints for more than one hour a week? If that's the state of our earthly souls, eternity is going to be a *long* time.

How on earth are we to be trained for the conflict of evangelism and the spiritual fight for holiness if we devote merely one hour out of 168 to training for Christ?

How can we resist the ideologies of the world if we aren't trained to identify them and to sniff them out and reject them?

Why is it that so many are deceived by the Prosperity Gospel? Because they aren't discipled.

Why are so many people prone to wander when they go away from the home church of their youth? Because we've made church a dating pool and social club rather than a bootcamp.

Why are so many people deceived by the false prophets of false religions? Because we haven't trained them up in the way that they should go but turned church into a playground of mindless entertainment, empty theology, and pointless procrastinations.

Why are so many unable to defend core doctrines like the Trinity, substitutionary atonement, the incarnation, and the authority of Scripture? Because we play with our faith rather than diligently obey Christ by being disciple-making disciples.

Why are so many unwilling to live a life of holiness, choosing instead the sexual revolution, choosing instead to kill children in the womb, choosing instead to wallow in the poison of addictions and destructive patterns, choosing instead to follow lying and corrupt politicians and vapid and empty celebrities? Because we haven't positively made the case for good, Godly living as a joyous expression of the gospel.

Why are so many distracted and deceived by social media stars and influencers, listening to lies on the distracting devices, often without a shred of critical thinking? Because we aren't discipling one another, allowing our peers in faith to mold us and challenge us and shape us. Because we're neglecting the Great Commission's command to exercise spiritual dominion in the kingdom of Christ.

We must avoid cheapening Christ's grace by assuming that *all* we do is 'believe' in Jesus but then keep on living like (and ultimately for) the devil. No. We are called to be conformed into Christ's likeness. We must grow in the family likeness. Our goal is to mature in our spiritual living.

And yes, there *is* freedom in the gospel. And, yes, we must avoid legalism and works-based religion. Christ has come to set us free from sin, shame, deception, and death. But that *leads* us to discipleship and a yearning to know our king and live under the constitution of his kingdom. If we simply treat Christ's gospel as a passport *out of Hell*, then we've misunderstood the *glory* and the breadth of the gospel. As P.T. Forsyth said, Christ did not "deliver us from evil simply to take us out of hell, [but to] take us into heaven." This means to be holy as God is holy. It means to reflect him to a fallen world that more might see and believe and join us in eternity with our holy God.

And thus I ask you, husband or wife: Do you know what your spouse reads for spiritual nourishment? Parents, do you know what your kids read for spiritual advice? Do you know what spiritual influencers they learn from on social media or in school or on YouTube?

What about you, Christian? Would *you* be *able* to identify a healthy teacher from a dangerous teacher? Would you be *willing* to help your brother or sister by showing them or teaching them? Christ has spoken and he *expects* you to both know and act in response to that knowledge. If we haven't spiritually matured since the day of our conversion then we are not being discipled and that means we are not disciples in a meaningful, practicable, sense.

Every single Christian is called, commanded, and commissioned to disciple *one another*. Let us, brother and sister, observe all that Christ has taught us and be faithful and obedient. So that during this interim, when Christ is on the throne in heaven, we won't be distracted by silly things like chronologies and timelines of the end. We don't know when Christ will return; we simply know that he will. And we *do* know what he *wants* from us in the meantime: To be evangelizing and discipling.

Therefore, let us go about his work with integrity, passion, and enthusiasm. Let's be disciple-makers. Imagine what your church and your community would look like if we were serious about the entirety of the Great Commission. What would change? How would your relationships, your attitude, and your actions change? How would your church outreach look? How might your church budget be better spent? How might church politics diminish and church unity develop?

Finally, we have seen that Christ also leaves us with the promise that he will never leave us nor forsake us. This is our encouragement to be obedient. He is all-powerful; we are going with his message... but we are also going *with* him. This means that we go with the message of Christ in the power of the Spirit of Christ who indwells us with the power of Christ. In one sense, Christ is *indwelling* us by his Spirit.

This means that we have the power to obey him. We have the power to share the gospel and the power to be a disciple-maker. This makes our excuses of being afraid, untrained, ill-equipped, or uncertain inadequate. The same Spirit who raised Christ from the dead now lives in you. You have power, authority, and ability when you rely upon the Spirit of Christ who is with you always. We *can* obey Christ through the Spirit, because the authority is matched by the presence of Christ through his Spirit. And this gives us confidence to the end of the age: He will never leave us nor forsake us.

But take a second and join the dots with me. Jesus told us to *obey* all His teaching. And then he said that he would be with us to the end of the age. We know he means that he will be present with us at all times through the indwelling of the Holy Spirit.

This promise *also* means that the words of Jesus? They are never going to pass away. Or come to an end. Or be replaced. In Deuteronomy? Moses told the Israelites to look for a new prophet and to listen to him. We saw that Jesus was that prophet on the Mount of Transfiguration. 'Moses' passes away, but the words of Christ do not.

Our Islamic friends claim that the New Testament is corrupted. But Jesus, here, tells us that his words are eternal, unchanging, and pure. They do not pass away. We continue to observe and obey them *until the end of the age.*

Our Mormon friends (and others) say that the New Testament was incomplete and that we need newer, final revelations. But Jesus, here, rejects that claim; he is the final word of God the Father. Any who adds to, or edits, his words, are rejecting his kingship.

Our progressive friends claim that we need to *reinterpret* Jesus for a modern context and to apply him in a way that we prefer today. Jesus, here, rebukes that view. His words are unending. They are pure and undefiled. We obey what he commanded us, *not* what our sinful desires *wish* he had said.

His teaching is the last and the final teaching for his kingdom. We don't need new prophets or priests or philosophies or ideologies or revelations or books or religions. We cling to Christ. We trust Christ. We grow in Christ. And we go with Christ.

To the end of the block. To the ends of the world.

And with every single step, he will be with us, never leaving us unprotected, unguarded or without his presence. He will never forsake us, leaving us isolated or alone. Why are we able to do this? Because *all* authority belongs to him. And we *trust* his power as well as his goodness.

And because Jesus reigns? The march of the king continues.

Through the feet of his church.

Until the end of the age.

The Sending Lord is the Returning Lord

[Acts 1:10] *And while they were gazing into heaven as He went, behold, two men stood by them in white robes,*

[11] *and said, "Men of Galilee, why do you stand looking into heaven? This Jesus, who was taken up from you into heaven, will come in the same way as you saw Him go into heaven."*

The Stranger Questions Their Gaze

The reason why the apostles left the mount is because they knew that the Lord *would* ultimately return. Yes, he may be ascending to his royal throne. And yes, he would send the Helper. But importantly, he had promised them, often, that he would return. And so, as they stood, mouths agape, catching flies? Two strangers, angels, were suddenly present in their midst.

And these strangers asked them: "Galileans? Why are you looking up? Why are you standing here just watching? Jesus was taken up from your presence into heaven."

Then what do they say?

"He'll *return* in the same way as you saw him go into heaven." In other words, they were saying: "Gentlemen. Take heart. This *isn't* the end of the journey. It's not the end of the story. The Lord *will* return." The implication is therefore that, until he returns, you have a task, a duty, a responsibility to fulfil. When the Helper comes, you'll be enabled and empowered to do it.

But notice the language in the middle of the sentence: "He will come *in the same way as you saw him depart*." This means that he will return visibly, dramatically, powerfully, and victoriously. His return will not be a secret. It will not be in stages. No; he will return, in might, to reign forevermore.

What a promise of hope. What a promise of joy.

Now, of course, there are almost innumerable interpretations of *how* we are to understand the chronology of Christ's return. Many big words are thrown around with extreme confidence: Dispensational premillennial, historic premillennial, amillennial, postmillennial, to name perhaps the most common. And these are all interpretations of the *timing* and, in some cases, the circumstances that lead to, Christ's return. But what no one denies, if they are Bible believing orthodox believers, is that, however you *interpret* the passages, the point is singular: Christ *is* returning. His return will be visible, it will be final, it will be victorious, and it will be consequential. Regardless of the various interpretations, Jesus *is* coming back, and this is cause both for celebration but also preparation.

Christian. Are you living in light of the Lord's return? Where are you investing your time? Where are you investing your money? How are you investing in your family? What about your relationships? How do you value your church community? Are you living *as if Christ is coming back*? Will he find you working for the kingdom? Or will he find you working for *your* kingdom? How might your life change if you truly realized and believed that this world, and this life is not the end, but merely the bootcamp, the training ground for the life to come? The kingdom of God is already here in part. But what is soon to come in totality is the true, eternal, and great reality of the finality of all things when God shall dwell with his people in their midst.

How might that conviction change your evangelism?

Penn Jillette once stated that he had *no respect* for a Christian who would not evangelize out of social anxiety or angst. Why? Because if we truly believed that Christ was coming and the *Hell* was the consequence for the lost, then we must either be *heartless* or filled with *hatred*, to not desperately desire that everyone we encounter avoid that reality. Dear brother or sister, *are you not captivated by the return of Christ?* Are you not *desperate* that every person hears the Gospel so that they can be *ready* for Christ's return? So that they can joyfully and willingly prostrate themselves in worship at his return rather than fear him and bend in terror as he righteously condemns the sinful rebel for spitting on the cross and remaining in their rebellion? Do we yearn to see the lost saved? No matter *who* they are: No matter their orientation, no matter their background, no matter their past, no matter their religion, no matter their apparent disinterest. We aren't called to *save* them, but we're commanded to *show* them the Savior.

All are welcome to the Master's table. Have we invited them?

Christ is returning. Are we obedient in the meantime?

And We Have A Purpose

Obedient, you ask?

[Acts 1:8] *But you will receive power when the Holy Spirit has come upon you, and you will be my witnesses in Jerusalem and in all Judea and Samaria, and to the end of the earth.*

Yes. In Acts 1:8 Jesus speaks to his apostles, and also to every single believer behind them because we all have the indwelling Holy Spirit. He tells us: "*You* will be my witnesses in Jerusalem and in all Judea and Samaria, and to the end of the earth." This is another version of the Great Commission. Just as he will be with us through the indwelling of the Holy Spirit to the end of the age, he sends us out to be making disciples to the ends of the earth. Because Christ is returning. And he will reign as the royal king over the New Creation.

But *until* then.

We are his ambassadors, his embassy to a lost and rebel world.

Are we being obedient? To make disciples for him? To evangelize and welcome people into his kingdom? And to help them become genuine, faithful, followers?

We have an incredible privilege. We're the advance party. We're the vanguard of the army of Messiah. We're the front ranks, marching across a rebel world, assaulting the gates of Hell in every corner of every sinful highway and every unrighteous ideology. Are we bringing the message of Christ to the world? Or are we so cold, so unloving, so callous as to not care that, as the hymn says, "souls are drifting into the night?"

Christ ascended to reign.

From his throne he sent the Helper.

But he is returning to judge.

And to rule over the earth.

Let us be ready. And let us be obedient in our quest to ensure others may be made ready with us.

Let us be about our Master's business. Until he returns home.

Conclusion

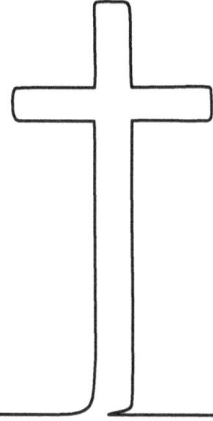

It is all '...because of Jesus.' I hope that as you've read through this short book on the incarnation, crucifixion, resurrection, and ascension of Christ, you've come to a deeper appreciation for what he has done for you.

It's because of Jesus that we can be reconciled our creator God even though we were born into rebellion and lived lives that resisted and rejected his rule and his grace. Jesus, the Word-made-flesh, is wholly God and wholly man. This truth is vital for us because it allows us to understand how God's wrath towards rebellious humanity could be satisfied without compromising his holiness or his mercy. Through the Lord Jesus, God punished sin by placing it on Jesus in our stead. We deserved sin and death and judgement; but God desired to offer mercy and grace and relationship. But our sin was a cavernous insult that horrified God's holiness and buried our own desire for forgiveness. We loved the darkness rather than the light and so we hid and reveled in the darkness. The world that God had created to so majestically display his glory had become a slimy pit of wickedness, evil, cruelty, torture, abuse, violence, and treachery. The glory of creation was dimmed by depravity.

This was why God chose to send Jesus. He is the Light of the World. Wherever he walked, God's grace and love penetrated through the gloom and the shadows with a blinding radiance of beautiful holiness. His kingdom expanded as he chose his disciples and taught them about the love of God and the kingdom that he was inaugurating. His kingdom was to stand in direct opposition to the kingdom of darkness. And it would bring life and light and a new paradigm of worship and relationship with God.

But the Realm of Man, the rebellion, soon recovered from the shock arrival of the king. Slowly, even as the light of his grace spread throughout Palestine, the darkness amassed its forces and prepared a brutal, vicious, and swift counterattack.

With the serpent nipping at the heels of Messiah, Jesus' enemies concocted a fabricated charge of blasphemy against him and then wheeled him into the palatial courts of the rulers of this world who, through personal ambition and political calculation, determined that it would be better to kill him than to risk enflaming a riot. Their calculation appeared correct; as suddenly as the Light had appeared, its glow was snuffed out. Scourged with extreme violence, abused at the hands of his own creatures, and brutally nailed to a wooden cross, Jesus, God-made-flesh, was murdered.

And the Light of the World was killed by the darkness of men.

The rebellion had triumphed.

Or had it?

Three days later, the Triune God acted to raise Jesus of Nazareth from the dead. This was no mere resurrection such as Lazarus or Jarius' daughter had experienced. Jesus was not simply *raised*, he was the *firstborn* of the New Creation. He was the firstfruits of a new harvest of citizens in his kingdom. His body was different. He looked similar, but not identical. He had metamorphosed into the prototype of a new humanity, a greater, a restored, a holier, a *redeemed* people.

Through his death, he had vanquished the rebellion by defeating the power of death, which was the consequence for our treason. He has borne that penalty in its fullness. But he has also assuaged and satisfied the justice of the holy God because he was an innocent, sinless, sacrificial victim, at the hands of men, and under the wrath of judgement. Through his death, our sins were atoned for, and our debts were cleared, and our rebellion was defeated.

By his resurrection, God demonstrated that he accepted Jesus' payment. God raised Christ in victory, showing that the penalty for sin had been paid and the privilege of adoption was now available. Salvation had been won. The Light was burning brighter than ever; and now the darkness was in retreat. Wherever the Light shines, the gates of hell shall not prevail against it. The war is over; there may be minor skirmishes, but the waves of time have shifted inexorably. Christ has won. Christ is reigning. Christ is king.

As the disciples watched, the resurrected Lord ascended into heaven whereupon he was crowned king of kings and seated at the right hand of God his Father. From there, even now, he rules and reigns in might and majesty. His followers are tasked with the glorious privilege of bringing the message of Christ to the world: The gospel. We get to bring the good news of victory, of glory, or restoration, or redemption, of joy to our neighbors. And that message is that Christ is exalted. He is reigning over all things now and forevermore.

And Christ is returning. He will return to consummate the kingdom he has inaugurated through his life, death, resurrection, and ascension. When he returns, the darkness that has been in retreat for millennia will collapse once and for all. Christ will crush the rebellion irreversibly. He will thwart all the wicked plans of his enemies, and he will reign as the Anointed King until he hands the peaceful, prosperous, and idyllic kingdom over to his Father who will be all in all.

And those of us who are in his kingdom by accepting his generous grace will be with him. We will finally fulfil that Creation Mandate that Adam so carelessly ignored. Death will be dead. Sin will be slain. Shame will be subjected. Sickness will be slaughtered. Satan and false religion will be in judgment. Tears will stop. Creation will be restored. Life will be eternal. Grace will be truly grasped. Joy will be inexpressible yet always on our lips. Worship will be genuine. And we will reign with him forevermore in perfect paradise where we shall be his people, and he shall be our God, and we shall see him as he is and know him face to face.

Because of Jesus.

www.ingramcontent.com/pod-product-compliance
Lightning Source LLC
Chambersburg PA
CBHW021237090426
42740CB00006B/572